HISTORIC TALES *of*
HIGHLANDS

HISTORIC TALES *of*
HIGHLANDS

LOOKING BACKWARD

HELEN HILL NORRIS

Foreword by Randolph P. Shaffner, Archivist Emeritus,
Highlands Historical Society

THE
History
PRESS

Published by The History Press
Charleston, SC
www.historypress.com

Front cover images: Helen Martense Hill Norris, granddaughter of Stanhope Walker Hill and Celia M. Edwards and a daughter of Frank Harrison Hill and Sarah Frost Hill. *Courtesy of Helen Hill Norris family*; Black Rock Mountain in Horse Cove. *Courtesy of Robin Phillips. Back cover images*: Hill House, Horse Cove. *Courtesy of Helen Hill Norris family.*

First published 2021

Manufactured in the United States

ISBN 9781467149457

Library of Congress Control Number: 2021934139

Notice: The information in this book is true and complete to the best of our knowledge. It is offered without guarantee on the part of the author or The History Press. The author and The History Press disclaim all liability in connection with the use of this book.

Dedicated to Helen Turner Lamb.

CONTENTS

Contents

CONTENTS

FOREWORD

S omeone has rightly said that the history of a country is a story of its people and their way of life." This is the reason Helen Hill Norris gave for writing this little book. It's a compilation of stories etched in her memory from when she was a child and told by her elders gathered around the fireside on many wintry nights.

A native of Highlands and Horse Cove in Western North Carolina, Helen wrote a column of these stories for the *Highlander* newspaper from its founding in 1958 until her death ten years later. A granddaughter of Highlands's first elected mayor, Stanhope W. Hill, and one of its first physicians, Dr. Charles Frost, she titled her column "Looking Backward" because it recorded little and big events of "back yonder," both true and folksy, that were treasured as amusing and intriguing.

With a great deal of authority and personality, the stories were told as true about the region's history, as evidenced by their titles: "The Law and the Mountain Women of the Early '90s," "The Talking Machine," "The Lost Gold Mine," "Wolfpack: 1885," "The Tooth Dentist Comes to Town," "Satulah Mountain Trembled," and "The Warwoman." One utterly charming tale even settles the argument "Does a Mole Have Teeth?"

When a reader of the *Highlander* complained that Helen should shift her focus to present-day Highlands or to the future rather than dwell so intently on the past, Helen defended herself, saying that she was writing about what she knew best, and her ardent fans agreed.

The line between history and folklore is sometimes blurred, but Helen's claim to truth is that this is how the stories were told to her in the vernacular of the mountain folks, whose creative and colorful tropes adorned their language like bright stars in the firmament.

On one occasion, Helen had an interesting visitor, "a type of pioneer woman born to the wilderness and wilderness ways," who spoke to her about Malviny Reid's "bad spell." As the woman finished her fascinating tale and wound her way homeward into the filtered glow of a rose-and-purple sunset, Helen pondered "the great individualism and human interest lore that abounds in these glorious mountains of ours."

Thanks to her descendants Robin Phillips and Luther Turner, these treasured tales are restored to print, along with photographs from the family archives. Readers can once again find as much pleasure inside these pages as they did when these stories were first written sixty years ago about happenings already eighty or more years old. Good stories of this type are timeless in the annals of well-written literature.

RANDOLPH P. SHAFFNER
Archivist Emeritus, Highlands Historical Society
Black Mountain, North Carolina
October 15, 2020

FOREWORD, OR THE REASON FOR THIS LITTLE BOOK

S omeone has rightly said that the history of a country is a story of its people and their way of life.

So it is, since our Highlands country holds within its rock-ribbed, beautiful plateau many little and big events of "back yonder" that are both amusing and intriguing, that I've decided to relate some of them in this little book, trusting that the reader will find as much pleasure inside these pages as I've enjoyed writing them.

It is with a bit of pride that I offer here only remembered tales, lots of them gathered around a fireside on many a wintry night while, as a child, I sat listening to my grandfather, my uncles, and my dad. These were the days when my ancestors, the Hills, owned all of Horse Cove.

I am indebted also to my mother, the late Sarah Frost Hill, who came here from her home in New York in 1878, and to whose memory,

Helen Martense Hill Norris, granddaughter of Stanhope Walker Hill and Celia M. Edwards, as well as daughter of Frank Harrison Hill and Sarah Frost Hill. *Courtesy of Helen Hill Norris family.*

along with my dad's, this little book is lovingly dedicated. I am also indebted to my sister, Mrs. Hazel Hill Sloan, for mentally recorded dates and data. And lastly, but not least, I am grateful to my friends here, both new and old, some of them treasured through the years that I've lived away from my homeland.

To all of these I attribute both inspiration and help for this little book.

HELEN HILL NORRIS
1960

ACKNOWLEDGEMENTS

From the outset, this has been a family affair. Thanks to Luther Turner, the author's grandson, and his wife, Ann, for their unfailing enthusiasm for this venture. Thanks to Robin Phillips, the author's grandniece, for spearheading the endeavor. The photos contributed from their personal archives enliven the stories. Thanks to Tyler Norris Trant, the author's great-great-grandson, for working with these old photos and making them presentable. Special thanks to Ruth Frost Schulte, the author's great-grandniece, for her faithful typing of the original manuscript and for her valuable advice regarding publishing. Thanks to Leigh Turner Trant, the author's great-granddaughter, and Kimberly Turner for the tedious but vital task of proofreading the manuscript, selecting the photographs to illustrate it and working with the publisher. And thanks to William Turner Lamb, the author's great-grandson, for editing the manuscript and helping bring Mama Helen's words back to life.

Our profound thanks to Kate Jenkins and Ryan Finn of Arcadia Publishing and The History Press for guiding us along the way.

A NOTE ON SOURCES

Information offered in footnotes about the locations of businesses and landmarks in Highlands comes from town records, from *Heart of the Blue Ridge: Highlands, North Carolina* by Randolph P. Shaffner (Faraway Publishing, 2004) and, in some cases, from memory. For information on historical references, we drew from authoritative websites, such as those of the *Encyclopedia Britannica*, the National Park Service and local historical societies, as well as contemporaneous news accounts.

INTRODUCTION

Helen Hill Norris was my grandmother's older sister. I knew her as Mama Helen. After her marriage to Frank Norris, she moved from Highlands, North Carolina, with her husband to Atlanta, where she raised her family. In the summers, to escape the Atlanta heat, she returned to the cool mountains with her children and, over time, their children to the Hill House, the family farm in Horse Cove, a valley southeast of Highlands in Western North Carolina. This is where I met her, for my family came to Horse Cove for the summers as well.

I remember Mama Helen as a spry, energetic woman of good humor who could commandeer the gaggle of nieces, nephews, and cousins for picnics at local swimming holes, complete with cast-iron skillets for making Peggy Hole pancakes. On sunny days, we children played in the numerous creeks throughout the Cove, hunting for smoky topaz, mica, or amethyst. The girls would make fairy pools in the creek while the boys turned over stones looking for rock worms. They would push the worms out, leaving the tubes for us to later make into necklaces and bracelets. There was no "technology." The phone was a party line—the ancient precursor to Facebook. TV reception was intermittent, with only rabbit ears for connection. And yet there was never a dull moment.

Mama Helen was a clever storyteller. On rainy days, we would gather on the broad Hill House porch and Mama Helen would tell stories of the joys, troubles, and adventures of growing up in Horse Cove in the late

1800s. Some of these stories are related here. I hope you enjoy them as much as I did, and still do.

ROBIN PHILLIPS
Grandniece of Helen Hill Norris

Helen Martense Hill Norris was born on November 5, 1882, in Highlands, North Carolina. She was one of four children of Sarah Frost Hill and Frank Harrison Hill. She married John J. Norris of Anderson, South Carolina, in 1901 and had four children of her own. She lived in Anderson; Greenville, South Carolina; and Atlanta, before returning to Horse Cove and Highlands. During her lifetime, she traveled cross-country to California in a Ford Model T, sailed on the Queen Elizabeth *to Europe with her two daughters and had a successful antique shop in Atlanta.*

LOOKING BACKWARD

THE LAW AND MOUNTAIN WOMEN OF THE EARLY '90S

Poems have been written, always carrying a bit of sentiment for the passing of old village and country schoolhouses. Last week's issue of the *Highlander* carried a notice pertaining to bids for wrecking and removing the old schoolhouse on the hill. The move will not be deplored by many since it falls under the name of progress—that relentless, ever-moving march for improvement—which is as it should be, for our very young nation is always on the move.

How-some-ever, there's some of we older ones who will feel a bit of sadness as memories come crowding in on the wings of sentiment when it passes. For instance, there's the time a foreign organ grinder, his portable organ on his back, with a monkey that danced to a gypsy tune wearing a little red coat and a cap, just broke up Miss Laura Belle's school. It was recess when the little monkey went around. Our little wondering eyes were a fascinated group, begging pennies, which of course in those days of little money were scarce. When he left, out went the whole school right behind him, following like the children in the pied piper story of old England. On we went, with Miss Laura Belle's admonitions of "Recess is over!," the sharp rapping with her ruler of no use at all. On we went, right down Main Street, until that bemused organ grinder stopped and put on another "show" for us.

Helen Hill Norris, age sixteen, *left*, with her niece Lizelle Willis and John J. Norris, circa 1898. *Courtesy of Helen Hill Norris family.*

How-some-ever, we soon became more local-minded as we met, of all things, Mrs. Smith, followed by Mr. Smith and the young'uns beating spoons on the backs of tin milk pans and ringing a dinner bell. They were after a swarm of bees who'd left the hive in their bee colony out on the Walhalla Road, following an old pioneer notion that the bee swarm would "settle" if enough noise was created. They did "settle"—the whole outfit on the back axle of Dock McKinney's ox wagon. By that time, here came Miss Laura Belle with the town marshal, and we were marched into order in no time flat.

Then, there came the day, way back yonder, when the town fathers, doing their best to enforce law and order in this rugged frontier, had built a small "calaboose," a word of Spanish origin meaning jail, across from the old schoolhouse* where the Sullivan property is now. It had fallen upon the town marshal to arrest and place therein two local characters who, in some small way, had run afoul of the law the night before. While we were all having our geography lesson, 'bout ten o'clock, here came the two culprits' wives. Can see 'em now, wearing wide calico skirts and sunbonnets and armed—one with a double-bitted axe across her shoulder and the other one with a double-barreled shotgun.

Lessons were forgotten then up at the schoolhouse on the hill. Out the windows and through the doors the boys went—needless to try to stop them. With one blast from her shotgun at the calaboose door hinges, after calling out to the men inside to "stay back," and a few blows following from the double-bitted axe, down came the door and out came the town's prisoners. And with no opposition whatsoever, back through town and out they went. True, the mayor—reckon it must have been old Dr. O'Farrell†—mildly came out as they passed his drugstore and tried to explain that the "law had been violated." The only answer he got as the procession strode belligerently by was from one of the women, who said, "You'uns can just leave our menfolk alone. We women up here tend to our men ourselves."

THE FIRST FLORIDIAN

I took to the open road the other day. Along with my young folks, the dog, and Betty the horse, I wandered down Walking Stick Road southward, following the creek. We passed the waterfall and swimming hole, hidden deep in the cavernous depths of the ravine through which the one big creek finds its way to the Chattooga River and on to the Atlantic Ocean.

Each turn showed a new vista, the little crooked, rocky road almost hidden in the lush growth of mountain evergreens, with an underlying carpet of ten varieties of fern and clinging moss on granite cliffs of many colors and kinds, challenging in their beauty the manmade moss gardens so famous in Japan.

Coming back and looking eastward to a lonely tall pine standing sentinel-like on a spur of Chestnut Mountain, it sort of hit me that, way up there

---

* Near the corner of Fourth and Pine Streets.

† Dr. Henry T. O'Farrell, who operated the Highlands Drugs store at the corner of Fourth and Main Streets, served as mayor of Highlands from 1887 to 1888, from 1890 to 1891, and from 1894 to 1900.

near the top, was built the first summer home by a Floridian. Mercy me, I thinks to myself, what an awful long time ago that was, for it was only hearing Grandfather tell about it that I can remember.

Sometimes the present-day Florida folks who spend many months with us ask if we had summer visitors before they came. It's no wonder, because it's only been in the past few decades that they've been coming. However, way back before the Civil War, the summer population consisted mostly of folks from Charleston, South Carolina; Savannah, Georgia; and New Orleans, as many fine old homes, still standing and restored by new owners, will testify.

William Patton, a wealthy cotton merchant, packed into a rugged spur of Mount Mitchell by slaves and ox team the material and furnishings for a commodious summer home long before the Civil War. There were many lovely summer homes built in the Highlands area as far back as the Civil War period. Most of them are gone now, among them the colonial home, the cabins for his slaves, his racetrack and racing stable, built by Judge J.N. Whitner of Anderson, South Carolina, whose beautiful home in Horse Cove was destroyed by Kirk's renegade army about 1864. The home was robbed of its valuables and burned to the ground.

My late Uncle Buck (Felix Grundy Hill) was a natural-born real estate dealer. Dad said he could sell a perpendicular mountain cliff. It was his custom to enter claims on land entries known as state grants for outlying forested tracts. Some of these grants are still in the family, signed by North Carolina's earlier governors John Morehead and Edward Bishop Dudley.

One could claim the land after registering with the land office in Raleigh. Then, upon building a fence around a cleared and cultivated field and upon payment of five dollars per hundred acres, a state grant could be obtained. So Uncle Buck, with an eye for business, had, as time went on, considerable holdings. Among them was the large tract of land on the lower reaches of Chestnut Mountain, down southward from our valley.

So it was that came along Herbert Allen of St. Augustine, Florida, in the 1870s, buying the land mentioned before that lay flat on the big western spur of the mountain from my uncle. Grandfather told me Mr. Allen built an exceedingly beautiful summer home there. Mother, who often visited the Allens after they came here, spoke many times of the luxurious Oriental rugs, bric-a-brac, silver, and paintings that went into its furnishings and how arduous the task must have been of transporting the heavy mahogany furniture and building material by ox team over the steep and muddy roads. The main road then from South Carolina into Highlands came through Horse Cove.

Home of Felix Grundy Hill (Uncle Buck) in Horse Cove. *Courtesy of Helen Hill Norris family.*

Well, the old Allen home is gone now, destroyed by a forest fire, furnishings and all, many years ago. All that's left are the remains of stone terraces, the lawns long since claimed by the forest. A lovely clear stream from the spring above the spot continues to find its way, circling the lawns and terraces as Mr. Allen trained its course, down the mountainside. The U.S. government now owns it.

BACK PORCH BOOKKEEPING

Being a retrospective sort, I got 'round to thinking the other day how little cash money we used to have. So it was that swapping and trading developed into a vital technique, and "buy" and "sell" were terms seldom heard.

A while back, when the children and I got together to work in earnest restoring the old home down in the Cove, I decided to get smart and brush down and clean the outside walls on our east terrace, which, before we took the roof off and cemented the floor, used to be a long screened back porch.

23

The author's father, Frank H. Hill, *seated*, and friends. *Courtesy of Robin Phillips.*

Busy with a steel brush, knocking off paint scales, I saw there in plain sight a record in Dad's handwriting, jotted down as though in a hurry. It reads as follows:

Aug. 6—'99

Leg of lamb

To Bill Toy for 2 bushels rye seed, to be picked up at Dryman's in the Flats.

Feb. 16

2 bushels seed potatoes to Alec Edwards for a pig when his sow comes in.

Nov. 6—'91

Let Mack Edwards have 1 quarter my stall-fed beef to be repaid when he butchers his.

To D.A. Watson—1 gal. molasses and 50 cents to buy his marriage license.

Advanced a loan, secured by note to Ernst Reid for two months rations and use of cabin under Black Rock for 1 year, provided he don't vote the Republican ticket this fall.

TEA AND TURNIP GREENS

Some time back, the *Highlander* published an interesting article with pictures of the old Stumphouse Mountain Tunnel. The tunnel, now owned by Clemson College for the purpose of curing cheese from its famous Dairy Department of Agriculture, was of pre–Civil War origin. Labor being scarce back in those days, quite a few Irishmen came over from the "old country" to work at digging the tunnel—a hard-sweating, hard-labor job, to say the least.

The crew had an English boss, and with the traditional Englishman's penchant for his cup o' tea, and not finding it in Walhalla, he proceeded to send back to England for it, ordering several pounds, which he thought would last for quite a while.

When it arrived, he turned it over to his cook at Walhalla's first pioneer inn, Beaman's Hotel, telling her to have it ready for him that evening. She did! When he came in, there it was—the whole five pounds of imported China tea, boiled up and laid out on a big platter with a chunk of "side meat" square in the center. When the dumbfounded Englishman confronted the cook, she said, "Lawsey, Mr. Patrick, I 'lowed you meant it to be cooked like turnip greens!"

THE TALKING MACHINE

Long before the present day of record players and tape recorders, long before the telephone reached into the mountains, amusement and attractions beyond the limited area of farm life were scarce.

Came a day once, though, that for one little family group was a red-letter day, indeed. That was always referred to afterward as "the day the talking machine man came." It was a windy March morning following a "snowed-in" winter. The valley then being without a post office for a while, Dad either sent our hired man, Sam, or rode himself to Highlands for the mail three times a week. The coming of the mail was in itself a day of quiet expectations, since it brought us kids the *Youth's Companion** and *St. Nicholas*† and magazines and papers for grown folks, all of which were read and talked over around the dining table and evening fireside. That was the winter Dad read aloud to us *The Adventures of Huckleberry Finn* and *Tom Sawyer*, and we children proceeded to name the new calves, sheep, and colts after characters in the two books. There was a mean ram in the flock of sheep that we promptly called "the Royal Nonesuch," etc.

That morning here came Sam post-haste in the east drive, so fast that Mother knew there was something in the wind.

"Any news from town, Sam?" she asked as she slammed the oven door on a batch of homemade bread and mincemeat pie and ran the cat out of the kitchen.

"Lan's yes, Mis' Hill, they's considerable," Sam said. "They's a man in town as has gone and got the head thing rigged up and sittin' up there on Dr. O'Farrell's drugstore front porch by the hotel, and it's one of them talking machines Mr. Hill's been readin' to us about, sure as God made little apples.

"Got a great big horn on it shaped kinda like a big morning glory, an' Mis' Hill," he said, dropping his voice to a whisper, "the dang thing talks and sings, and there's the awfulest crowd of folks gathered up around it, and bringin' in folks to Dr. O'Farrell's drugstore buying barlow knives and rock candy and smokin' tobacco. Why, you ain't never seen such a crowd since the circus tried to come to town an' the elephant and the circus wagons got stuck in the mud coming up Pine Mountain an' the clowns had to all get out

---

* The *Youth's Companion* was a magazine for children and families published in Boston from 1827 to 1929, when it was acquired by *American Boy.*

† *St. Nicholas* was a monthly literature magazine for children, published from 1873 into the 1940s.

Sarah Apalonia Frost, daughter of Dr. Charles L. Frost and wife of Frank Harrison Hill. *Courtesy of Helen Hill Norris family.*

an' push, an' the lions all got to roarin' and scared all the critters around 'til they took off for the Smokies."

We young'uns all stood around wide-eyed and begged Mother to take us to see and hear the talking machine, of course.

How-some-ever, that windy March morning turned out to be a memorable one, for looking out the window we saw the "peddler woman" comin' across the field patch from Uncle Buck's carrying samples of the then-new aluminum cooking ware. Her coming was always a field day anyway, for often she spent the night, bringing news and choice neighborhood gossip from the countryside.

And many fine tales she spun as she sat by the fireside, Mother giving her an order while she cut a wedge of hot mince pie and poured a cup of coffee for her. Suddenly there was a commotion in the yard, and looking out, there was the "talking machine man" in person, machine and all!

Mother, wildly excited, said to me, "Run fast up under the mountain and tell your father and Sam to come quick, the talking machine man's here. They're up there getting firewood. Hurry." And she went into the dairy room off the kitchen for a pitcher of cream.

By that time, the machine was being placed on the table in the kitchen and Mother, being of a somewhat frugal turn of mind, started getting the least bit suspicious and asked the man, "How much to play it?" And to us, in a low tone, she said, "Such a wonderful device can't possibly be for free."

"Well now Miss Hill" 'lows the man, "this here thang, it cost a sight of money—moreover, this thang it won't play for anybody but me."

"Why?" said Mother. "All you got to do is wind up that handle on the side, put one of these round cylinders in it, and it starts playing and all those little needles on the cylinders begin moving. I've read all about them."

"Well now, Miss Hill," he says, "all I got to say is that it's my talking machine and I've got to charge everybody as listens to it 25 cents apiece or I don't play it."

Mother did some quick thinking then, money being scarcer than hen's teeth and not growin' on trees. "Look," she says, "there's eight of us and this lady agent makes nine. I'll send over the field-path for my nieces, and that all

This piano was a graduation gift to Sarah Frost from her great-uncle Gideon Frost in June 1878. She had finished her education at Quaker College in Locust Valley, Long Island, New York. When Sarah moved with her father, Dr. Charles L. Frost, to Highlands, the piano was sent by railroad from New York to Seneca, South Carolina. It took six mules, four men and three days to bring it to Highlands. *Courtesy of Helen Hill Norris family.*

adds up to twelve. Then I'll give you two dollars and your dinner, and Sam, the hired man, will feed your horse. How's that?"

For a little while then, the old farmhouse kitchen, filled with the fragrance of Mother's home-baked bread, became for us the music center of the universe as the strains of "Home Sweet Home," "Swannee River," "The Mockin Bird" and Bro. Talmadge's "Sermon on the Bible" came floating from the big morning glory horn of the talking machine.

That, as I said, was a real red-letter day. The peddler lady and her aluminum ware and the talking machine man were invited to spend the night. Toward late evening they were joined by the piano tuner, who came up once a year to tune Mother's Steinway grand,* which had been brought up from Seneca, South Carolina, by a six-mule team and was the first piano to ever reach the Highlands area. The trip took three days, changing teams twice on the way.

---

*The piano is a Chickering square grand piano.

We young'uns were allowed to stay up late that night, the piano tuner and the other two travelers being company. We sat up 'til all hours around the fire in the east living room while the travelers regaled us with many a fine tale.

Ah, those dear days so well remembered!

How Cashiers Got Its Name

It's a rather odd name, some folks think.

According to an old record, Highlands really owes its location to the fact that its founders, S.T. Kelsey and Arthur Hutchinson,[*] were unable to buy enough land for their remarkable enterprise at the right price for development.

Well, looking backward into some remarkably authentic records, it seems General Andrew Pickens,[†] after retirement from his service as an officer in the American Revolution, built a manor house on a large plantation in upper South Carolina at Tamassee, where the DAR School is now located, in the county that still bears his name. It became his custom to send big herds of cattle, horses, sheep, hogs, and even great flocks of turkeys up into the lush mountain valleys for grazing during the hot, dry South Carolina summers. Having two obstreperous prize bulls in his herd, General Pickens—in a humorous trend, I reckon—named them after two ancient Roman senators, Cassius and Brutus.

Cassius, when brought down in the fall to the plantation, would nearly always break pasture and return to "the valley," as it was then known and still is by some of the older residents. So General Pickens and his men fell into the way of calling it "Cassius Valley," and by and by folks sort of fell into the way of saying "Cash's Valley." And finally along someone came who, not knowing the origin of the name, added "i-e-r-s," and it became Cashiers, a misnomer for the original name, as so often happens with the passing of time.

---

[*] The town of Highlands was founded by Samuel Truman Kelsey and Clinton Carter Hutchinson. Legend has it that they drew two straight lines on a map—one from Chicago to Savannah, Georgia, and the other between Baltimore and New Orleans—and established Highlands where they intersected, figuring that it would become a crossroads for commerce.

[†] During the American Revolution, Andrew Pickens (1739–1817) was one of the more important leaders of Patriot forces in the South Carolina backcountry, commanding the state's militia to a decisive victory over British and Loyalist forces at the Battle of Cowpens in January 1781.

And then, over nearer to the South Carolina line, a pioneer log cabin settlement—now deserted and returning to the forest—was named Bull Pen, all because the general's herdsmen used the place for a bimonthly "salting ground" and built some log pens to hold up and count the fall roundup of cattle.

There are other tales as to how Cashiers got its name, of course, but the above is from pre–Civil War records from one of the valley's first settlers, and I believe it to be correct.

It's interesting to know that Cow Rock, rising directly above the lake at Sapphire Valley Inn, as well as Sheep Cliff and Hog Back, are all names left by the general's herdsmen.

There's Turkey Ridge, too, for many early settlers besides the Pickens outfit turned their droves of turkeys loose with bells to fatten on the huge chestnut crop. Sometimes as many as two hundred were known to be in one flock. And Horse Pasture River, that clear and beautiful stream that flows southward into the lower reaches of upper South Carolina over the highest waterfall in our section. And Whitewater. That river was named also because the Pickens horses used to graze there, and it became known as Horse Pasture Country.

Seems those must have been pretty easy days, what with a feller's stock living off the fat of the land, so to speak—the free range. I guess this area around here was about the last to come under the state law of discontinuing open range for livestock. And I guess, too, my late father, Frank H. Hill, came under severe criticism from his neighbors when he advocated the passing and enforcement of the Stock Law, closing the open range and providing that all livestock be kept under fence. Dad became quite unpopular, I'm afraid, for then everyone had large herds of cattle, sheep, and hogs that could feed and graze on open range from May through September. No one who has ever tasted hog meat fattened on wild chestnuts—dressed and ready to bring home from the forests, ready to cure—can ever forget the flavor.

Yes, it sure was easy livin'. The way my folks used to call the sheep down the mountain from the back of our house about every two weeks for a roundup and a "salting," generally late afternoon on a Saturday, was an unforgettable scene—as many as a hundred sheep coming single file on a narrow trail down the mountainside, led by an old "bellwether" to the barnyard below, answering Dad's call with an occasional bleat. Somehow, the scene seems almost biblical. I reckon Dad must have been looking ahead to the future of the forests even then, for soon came the U.S.

Whiteside Mountain. *Courtesy of Robin Phillips.*

government to back him up in the Stock Law, with the establishment of the great Nantahala National Forest.

As for me, I still would dearly love it the way it used to be: following open cattle trails through the woods and riding on horseback down to the Valley of Mystery, in the upper Chattooga River country, with my Uncle Grundy to count and give salt to his herd of horses at the salt ground known as the Big Stomp. Nearby, the "lettered log," with Civil War General Wade Hampton's* name carved on it, sat where the general used to hunt deer while a guest at our old original home in Horse Cove.

THE LOST SCOTCHMAN

There was a time once, when our nation, emerging from English control as a colony into our present and growing independence, that for some strange and seemingly uncalled-for reason, it became the custom of the mother

---

* Wade Hampton (1818–1902) was a lieutenant general in the Confederate cavalry, serving as second in command to General J.E.B. Stuart. He later served as governor of South Carolina and represented the state in the U.S. Senate.

country to send her young men to America—sometimes for political reasons, sometimes because of family differences. The older sons of many of England's and Scotland's very best families were considered more favorably in line of inheritance, titles, and the like, so it was often the case that younger sons were sometimes sent to the colonies to seek their fortunes—to Australia and India, both under British rule then, and to America.

They became known in the U.S. as "remittance men," since their families sent a monthly remittance in the way of a check for living expenses. Two such men, Redford Hope and Charles Wield of England, once owned the whole of Horse Cove and were true gentlemen of the highest order—graduates of Eton College and Oxford University.

Sometimes one tries to separate fact from fancy—with a "smidgen" of myth and folklore thrown in—but so far this little homespun column has stuck to facts handed down through past generations. So it is with this story of the "Lost Scotchman." Though somewhat veiled in obscurity, it is substantiated to this day down along the rugged region of the Chattooga River country through such names as Scotchman's Creek, shown on the forestry maps and not shown by any other. And there is the old cattle range country known locally as "Glen O'Wherry," as Scotch as heather and Scotch scones! It's a wild and broken country, the Chattooga, ages ago making its way through barriers and falling gradually away southward to lower levels. And it was here, back when there was free range for stock, that every May my folks took their droves of cattle, horses, and hogs down to Glen O'Wherry, for there was lush grazing in the sheltered valleys between the high ridges.

I used to ride down there on horseback with Grandfather, Dad, and my brother to round up the stock and count them, calling them up from way over the hills and valleys to the salt-lick grounds. It was a picturesque scene, with Dad sitting straight on old Charlie, his saddle horse, while he called, in his strong, beautiful voice, the cattle and horses in, pausing and motioning me to keep quiet as he listened for the first knock of the cow bells followed by a steady *tink-tink* as they struck the trail coming in for salt. Once he showed me the "lettered log" where a long time ago, using the spot to "stand" deer hunting, names had been carved—among them being General Wade Hampton, later a governor of South Carolina, who was often a visitor to Grandfather's and for whom High Hampton in Cashiers was named. Childlike curiosity getting the best of me, I fell to wondering, asking questions as to why it was called "Glen O'Wherry." I read up on the Scotch dialect, concluded it was "Oh, Glen, where am I?" and through usage had fallen into a more Americanized version or translation.

Working on the Hill House farm. *Courtesy of Helen Hill Norris family.*

"Well," said Grandfather, one day riding along the trail, "he was a true Scotchman, that fellow. Some of us found him down here all beat out and hungry and tired, for he'd been lost. He said the best he could make out for a week, and it was getting along toward winter and cold—he'd hardly say anything we could understand, us not being used to his broad Scotch—but now and then he'd mutter something like, 'Oh, Glen, wherra am I?'

So that's how come that name, and that's how come Scotchman's Creek. He disappeared—gone next morning—after I'd carried him home to Grandmother. Don't know where he went or what—his bed was empty when we called him for breakfast—but he was a true gentleman at that, if I ever saw one. Think he must have lost his mind a little all those days trying to find his way out. Might have been a 'remittance man.' Who knows?"

WHITESIDE: A MOUNTAIN OF MYSTERIES

While all of us are familiar with the strange and beautiful mountain that lifts its 4,930 feet of forest-clad and stone-faced cliffs from the Highlands plateau, and while many tourists driving up the well-graded road to the parking area pause for a while to drink in the different views, many do not know that there have come down through the passing years from hand to mouth, so to speak, interesting facts connected with it.

There's the last frontier for the bears. Back in the 1870s, old Mr. Barak Norton, one of the first settlers, would sit out on Bear Trail on cold nights in the late autumn, before the bears hibernated for the winter and as the sharp, cold winds were howling. He'd bury his feet in the earth to keep warm, wait patiently 'til the bear came back down the mountain through what the pioneers called the "White Side Laurel," and nearly always got his bear. In fact, he was a good shot, hardly ever known to miss, and his larder was well stocked all winter with fresh meat.

And then there's the story, picked up from a conversation not too long ago with a naturalist, that Chimney Top—that tall one lying back of High Hampton over Cashiers way—was, listen to this, at one time back in time, when the oldest mountains in the world were young, a part of Whiteside Mountain. In the great upheaval when the mountains were born, and chaos reigned—maybe taking centuries, no one knows—Chimney Top split from the eastern face of Whiteside Mountain, leaving the great mile-high stone face with its caves and cliffs, forming a scene of bewildering beauty.

From the top—reached by trails and jeep train from the parking area, and jutting outward, suspended over the awesome drop of several hundred feet—is Fools Rock, and it got its name in a very odd way. Dad went on a picnic once as a small boy with a crowd of boys and girls up on the mountain, and a venturesome girl in the crowd led her horse around the trail up from the campground, now a real estate development. She went around "Fat Man's Squeeze" (you have to climb a ladder to go that way now) and led the horse on up to the top. Her name was Ivy Simmons; she was a beautiful blonde and an expert horsewoman who was visiting her uncle and aunt, the H.B. Sellecks, from up North somewhere. She rode her horse straight out on Fools Rock and, with no room to turn the horse around, backed it step by step slowly back to the trail while the others in the party sat spellbound, almost afraid to breathe. Dad said it was a picture he'd never forget: Ivy, slender and beautiful, wearing a black velvet riding habit, sitting on her horse, suspended on one slender rock over space. One misstep would have meant sudden death. It's been called Fools Rock ever since.

Prowling around on the old mountain one day some years back, I came across a hideout of some sort. Following a trail leading off from the old campground, I came upon a sort of huge overhanging boulder. The trail seemed open, leading around the rock, and to my utter surprise, there was a boarded-up room, built of rough bark slabs, with the overhanging rock for a roof. There was a door on rusty hinges and, upon opening it, I saw an old rusty iron stove, a frying pan and kettle, and, loads of all things, piles of old magazines. Someone, evidently of a literal turn of mind, had surely "holed in" there for a long time, because there was a bunk bed with an old

Whiteside Mountain is 4,930 feet high and one of the oldest mountains in the United States. *Courtesy of Robin Phillips.*

worn blanket. There's a story that someone running afoul of the law had hidden away there all one winter.

Be that as it may, Whiteside Mountain, the mysterious one, still guards the secret, as she does the tale told by a man still living in Highlands of encountering an old Cherokee Indian out west, back in the '90s, who told him his people, when they were removed to Oklahoma during the horrible "Trail of Tears," were led from Horse Cove around through Whiteside Cove, beyond and up Whiteside Mountain. The Cherokee said that one of the tribe secretly carried a buckskin bag of gold and that they buried it on the mountain as the leader, a white man, passed out of sight around a bend of the trail, thinking, poor things, that they would probably come back someday and get it. Still, old Whiteside guards the Indian's secret hiding place, guards it as she does many other secrets.

HIGHLANDS' FIRST DRUGSTORE

There was a time when Dr. H.T. O'Farrell's drugstore, the first in Highlands, stood where Frank Cook's real estate office is now, where the kindly, voluble little Irish doctor dispensed castor oil, paregoric, horse liniment, and worm medicine; made his own pills; and attended to the ills of the town's populace back in the '80s and '90s.

Dr. O'Farrell was a devoted Episcopalian, one of the first vestrymen of the Church of the Incarnation, and for many years the leader of the church's choir. He was so proud of the church's first prayer books and hymnals that often after each service he carried them all home with him in a big market basket for safekeeping.

There'd be choir practice at the O'Farrells' bright and cheerful home twice a month on Friday night when Mrs. O'Farrell would serve her delicious New England doughnuts and coffee. Afterward, Mrs. O'Farrell and the doctor usually wound up the choir practices in a heated argument over the doctor's sounding off with his tuning fork, from which she was expected to pick up the right note for the piano accompaniment. So we'd have to wait, sitting primly on the Victorian horsehair sofas and chairs 'til things died down and the argument was over, although at times it waxed exceedingly strong.

Among other memories, Luther Rice always opened his butcher shop on Fridays and Saturdays in the off-season in a neat little screened-in,

Sarah Frost Hill and a family friend. *Courtesy of Helen Hill Norris family.*

sawdust-covered building in back of the W.S. Davis General Store, a rock building where the Hotel Edwards is now.* Luther would let it be known by word of mouth just what meat would be available, mostly native beef and lamb, and it was delicious!

Claude McCall used to sell groceries in back of Jim Hicks's barbershop where the Highlander Restaurant is now located.† That was next to Bennie's Pool Room.

And there was a time when the cashier of the Jackson County Bank, located where Jellen's Gem shop is now,‡ being a registered pharmacist,

---

* The current site of the Old Edwards Inn and Spa, at the southeast corner of Fourth and Main Streets.

† Formerly the Hicks Building, at 370 Main Street.

‡ No. 201 South Fourth Street, the current site of the Highlands Gem Shop.

not only attended to the bank's affairs, but went over to the drugstore to fill prescriptions, too!

Funny how times change. Those were friendly, do-it-yourself days. Oftentimes one would see some of the help at hotels walking across the street with a glass-oil lamp in each hand to be filled with kerosene at the Bascom's Store,* and what a store that was! If there was a thing that Henry Bascom didn't keep there, it just wasn't to be had—from a glass-covered showcase that held gumdrops, stick candy, rock candy, and chewing gum, to the back of the store where hung milk buckets, horse collars, plow lines, and whatever!

And then there was Mr. T. Baxter White, Highlands' first postmaster, who brought his family here from Shelburne, Massachusetts, in the late '70s. He maintained a New England–type store that now has its counterpart only in a TV setting. Mr. White had his post office in the building where Dr. Jessie Hedden's dental office is now,† and on the wall by the door hung the first telephone to come to Highlands. It was the talk of the town, with everybody coming in to see it and talk to Walhalla, South Carolina, the only outside connection.

So now comes the space age, with America's Pioneer V rocket "talking back" to us from eight million miles out. "Talking to the Jodrell Signal Station in England,‡ and relayed back to the U.S., reports that the rocket transmitted 64 items of information a second"—in code, of course.

One wonders sometimes just where and what we're headed for in this rapidly changing world—wondering and groping, childlike, for a sense of security. May be one reason why we are prone to look backward and cling to a love of the "good old days."

THE LOST GOLD MINE

There's a trite old saying among gold prospectors that "gold is where you find it." They used to roam the mountains when I was a child—gentle old men with a pick and shovel and a "gold pan," which was a large, rather flat,

---

* No. 114 North Fourth Street, currently the site of Highlands Sotheby's International Realty.

† The current site of the Town Square shopping area on Main Street.

‡ The Jordell Bank Observatory, about twenty miles south of Manchester, England, is home to a steerable radio telescope, one of the world's largest, that was used as part of the tracking network for the U.S. space program.

and shallow metal pan in which branch gravel or dirt was "washed," the gold falling to the bottom of the pan after the water had washed away the sand. Sometimes looking like the prospectors from the Klondike of 1898, they'd lead a mule bearing their "outfit" for roughing it and their "grubstake."* Be that as it may, once—just once—they "struck it rich." That would be back long 'bout 1896.

Came along from somewhere in North Georgia a red-headed, freckled-faced young feller—sort of a quiet guy. Being used to inquiries about old "gold diggers," and I reckon it being spring and corn-planting time, no one paid much attention to him. So he sort of disappeared down toward the Chattooga River country. But all at once things broke loose! Hitting a piece of gold-bearing quartz, small handfuls of little gold nuggets fell under his awfully surprised eyes! More quartz continued to produce gold, but of all things, that fellow just filled his pockets and knapsack and disappeared. I've never known for sure what became of him.

Came by the grapevine way of getting news then that the "find" was on land owned by the late Bishop Hugh Miller Thompson of the Episcopal Diocese of Jackson, Mississippi. He had acquired several hundred acres of wild outlying mountain lands during the years when he and his family built and maintained a summer residence in Horse Cove. He was the maternal grandfather of Colonel James H. Howe of Horse Cove. "The Bishop," as he was known by local people, was beloved by everyone who came in contact with him, and it was in Horse Cove that he wrote many of the textbooks that I've been told are still used at the University of the South at Sewanee, Tennessee.

Well, seems the Bishop, down at his home, Battle Hill, in Jackson, Mississippi, took a dim view of the discovery of gold on his land. He didn't take it too seriously, and things dragged along. I'm told that local people finally obtained a mineral lease from the Bishop and subleased it to three men who had investigated and tunneled into the ridge where the discovery was made. These men were from Georgia and were only able to obtain a very short lease, but they hired a lot of help. They kept guards at the mine day and night, and I remember my father and mother coming home from a trip to the mine one Sunday afternoon telling of the guard at the mine taking them inside the tunnel and showing them the clear white and amber quartz, studded with gold nuggets. Terribly excited, everybody was!

Time was running out fast on the three men's lease (I remember their names but must withhold them), and they were still digging further into the

---

* Money or supplies advanced to a prospector in return for a share in any findings.

Frank H. Hill, *kneeling*, with his daughter Hazel Hill Sloan, *far right*, and her husband, Willet Sloan, around 1919. Their daughter Sally Sloan is at center. *Courtesy of Robin Phillips.*

ridge as the gold-bearing quartz continued to lead them on. Finally they put on a night-and-day shift, working around the clock, crushing by hand with sledgehammers and "go-devils,"[*] running them through the "riffles,"[†] some of which were wooden troughs, with little cross-slats coated with quicksilver to hold the gold as the water ran through the crude troughs on the branch below the mine.

So it was that about three weeks before their rights expired they began hauling their rich quartz to a spring at Grandfather Hill's home, which they

---

[*] A rotary tool for scraping out obstructions.

[†] A shallow section of a stream.

used as a residence during the "Gold Rush," and there, after the option had expired, they worked for a long time, crushing and beating up the gold-bearing quartz, washing it through the water, and taking it away with them: nuggets of the purest gold!

We children, after they left, would go to the rock pile they left, and even years afterward, my brother-in-law T.W. Norris of Anderson, South Carolina, picked up enough gold to make his daughter a class ring, as well as several pairs of cufflinks for himself.

And then Mother Earth, guarding as she has and does her secrets from exploitation, decided enough was enough! Suddenly the gold-bearing quartz gave out, and through the following years and decades no amount of labor and gold-digging has ever yielded so much as a grain of gold dust. There are those who surmise that the "lead" would open up further on, but geologists who are "in the know" doubt it.

So the "lost mine" rests, guarding its secrets well, the old tunnel caved in and barely noticeable now. It is covered by nature's beauty of laurel, and along with long-ago stirring events of the mountains, perchance, remembering when once it yielded $60,000 worth of precious gold in a few short hours, it sleeps silently through the years.

GRANDFATHER'S BEAVER HAT

They used to tease Grandfather terribly, Dad said, about his "beaver," or silk tall hat. Kept him busy trying to explain he only had it by an accident. Had no truck, he said, with tall hats; they belonged to statesmen and the "higher-ups" and the like, and he clung fondly to his old wide-brimmed southern planters black felt.

Anyway, seems that during the Civil War my uncle, who had been badly wounded at the Battle of Seven Pines in Virginia,[*] was home on sick leave. After his recovery, he was ordered back into service at Charleston, South Carolina, and Grandfather decided to go along with him. While passing through Belton, South Carolina, on the train, Grandfather lost his hat by sticking his head out of the car window, much to his loss of dignity. He proceeded to have the conductor hold up the train while he went out to

---

[*] Also known as the Battle of Fair Oaks, the Battle of Seven Pines was a two-day Civil War battle fought east of the Confederate capital of Richmond, Virginia, in 1862. The Union position held, although both sides suffered heavy casualties.

Felix Grundy Hill, known as Uncle Buck, was a son of Stanhope Walker Hill and Celia Edwards Hill. One of nine children, he was born in 1840 and grew up in Highlands. When the Civil War broke out, he enlisted and fought under the command of General Joseph E. Johnston. Uncle Buck was wounded at the Battle of Seven Pines near Richmond, Virginia. Stanhope found him in a hospital there and brought him home to recuperate, paying a man fifteen dollars per month to take Uncle Buck's place. After about three months, he returned to his regiment, which was then in Eastern North Carolina. At war's end, he walked home the length of the state barefoot, his uniform in tatters, carrying a Minié ball (a type of bullet) that had recently been removed from his knee. That Minié ball stayed on his mantel or in his pocket and was buried with him at the Horse Cove Cemetery. Uncle Buck loved to tell tall tales and vowed that he was the only Buck private in the whole Confederate army. Everyone else, he said, was a captain or a colonel. After this, his friends started calling him Buck, and his nieces and nephews took to calling him Uncle Buck. He married Ursula Alley, a daughter of Colonel John H. Alley of Whiteside Cove, who had fought in the Mexican-American War. Uncle Buck and Ursula raised a fine family, but none chose to stay in the area. One daughter, Lizelle, went north to study nursing and returned home with her husband-to-be. They were married in the parlor of the old home, but Uncle Buck refused to give her away because she was marrying a Republican. *Courtesy of Helen Hill Norris family.*

The Tallulah Gorge railroad trestle. *Courtesy of Helen Hill Norris family.*

buy a new one. The idea of holding up a whole trainload of soldiers for a hat! Seems the only thing he could find was a tall, black silk one, three sizes too large at that, but back into the train he goes, hat and all, with the hat resting square on top of his ears.

Assuming such dignity as was possible, and amid the lighthearted bantering shouts of the soldiers aboard—"Come down out of that hat, old man, we see your feet hanging out"—he allows to my uncle, "Just listen to those fool boys, Buck. It's a good thing I can't hear 'em." He was supposed to be stone deaf.

Speaking of the conductors holding up that train, it reminds me somewhat of the time I was going back to Atlanta, driving down to Dillard to catch the southbound Tallulah Falls train,* and found I'd missed it. "Don't worry a bit," says Mr. Coffey, the station agent. "I'll call down to Mountain City and tell the conductor to wait for you."

With my brother Harry driving, we took off in great haste, with me amazed at having a train wait for me. But there it was, puffing and blowing, the conductor out on the step of the passenger coach waiting for me. To

---

* The Tallulah Falls Railroad opened in 1881 and was later extended to a fifty-eight-mile route from Cornelia, Georgia, to Franklin, North Carolina. Financial trouble and a series of accidents led to its closure in 1961.

add to my embarrassment of having a train held up, he calls down to the engineer, who had his head out of the window, doubtless thinking, "Ain't that just like a fool woman to hold up my train?" The conductor calls to him and allows, "Back this train a little, Joe. How do you expect a lady to get on this train in a mud puddle?"

We older ones are somewhat saddened by the loss of that little railroad. Sometimes, on clear autumn days when the wind was from the West, we could hear the train's whistle as it left Franklin for the afternoon run down to Cornelia, Georgia. But out among the files of moving picture "takes" in Hollywood is Walt Disney's "The Great Locomotive Chase,"* so in a way the old railroad history has been preserved, for it was staged—all of it—on the Tallulah Falls Railway!

MOUNTAIN MEDICATION

Yes, you're expected to eat poke "salet"† (not "salad" if you're true mountain-born), for long 'bout this time o' the year, the womenfolk begin looking here and yonder—where a brush heap has been burned or round in sheltered fence corners—for the luscious vegetable. Brought home, the tender young shoots are carefully washed, boiled for about fifteen minutes in clear water, drained, and then cooked slowly in bacon drippings or butter and served with hard-boiled eggs grated over the top. It's a right good dish—calculated, according to the settlers who learned much from the Indians, to be an excellent tonic along with sassafras tea and things like that. Well, they kept pretty healthy, the old-timers.

There was tea to be made from yellow root now flowering along the trickling stream's banks—that was for a sore mouth—and cornmeal made into a poultice‡ for "drawing" the inflammation from a sore spot. There was arbutus tea for kidney ailments and the tender-side bark from a white oak tree made into tannic acid for burns. And long before mountain mothers knew of even Mennen's talcum powder for their babies, an Indian

---

* A 1956 film starring Fess Parker and based on real events in which Union soldiers attempt to bring an early end to the Civil War by crippling the Southern railroad network.

† Poke salet (also "sallet") is a dish consisting of cooked pokeweed, a perennial weed found in abundance in Appalachia and across the South. Pokeweed is poisonous, but when properly cooked, its leaves and stems are a good source of protein, fat and carbohydrates.

‡ A hot, soft, moist mass of flour, herbs, or mustard—for instance, spread on cloth and applied to a sore or inflamed part of the body.

Helen Hill Norris, *left*, with her daughter Dorothy Norris Turner in Horse Cove. *Courtesy of Robin Phillips.*

squaw showed them how to take the dry powder like dust from under a fallen pine tree, tie it into a little thin piece of cloth and cure up the chafed skin on little bodies.

One cold November morning, when my little baby sister, at six months, was desperately ill from what we later knew as colitis, Mother, in desperation and not having a doctor to call in from anywhere 'round, sent me galloping off on my horse for old Mrs. Wiggington, about a mile down the road. Seems when Mother didn't know what to do in an emergency with us youngsters, she always sent for Mrs. Wiggington.

Assured by my childlike assertion that the baby was near about dead—Mrs. Wiggington, the old soul whom neither height nor depth nor nothing above or underneath the earth ever in the least way shook out of her composure—took a mattock,* quietly went across the creek and dug up some roots of a plant she called "angelico." We got on my horse and here we took off riding double. Getting there, she proceeded, still with no comment, to build up the kitchen stove fire and make tea from the angelico. She took the convulsive, stricken baby in her broad lap and dosed her now and then with the tea. Believe it or not, in two hours the fever was gone, and the wracked little body quiet and relaxed.

One time our old cow Brindle choked at feeding time on turnips cut up with the cotton seed meal. Came the familiar yell for Dad, who'd called in the neighbors, and in spite of all they could do, it looked like old Brindle wasn't going to make it. "Send Helen on Molly for old Mrs. Wiggington," Dad said. Away again, Major and our dogs bringing up the rear, and again (ah, the resourcefulness of pioneer life), all Mrs. Wigginton said was, "Your Mammy got any soft lye soap in the soap barrel?"

"No'm," I say. "But hurry, Mrs. Wiggington, Brindle's choking!"

Grabbing up a gallon bucket, she dashed out to the smokehouse and, taking a dipper, filled the bucket with the liquid ropey stuff. And away again, me holding on to the bucket of soap. Getting there, what did she do but mix the soap with warm water and, going out to the barn lot, held up both of Brindle's big ears and poured it down her ears, inside! Upon which the old milk cow, shaking her head like anything, began coughing and up came the turnip. The soapy water running down her throat and ears I reckon did it.

Mrs. Wiggington was a firm believer in keeping a lump of asafetida† tied around her children's throats to keep off colds, no doubt making them very unpopular with their friends. Molasses and sulfur for a spring tonic. But she raised eight healthy men and women in spite of it all.

THE NEW BABY WAS A GIRL

'Bout this time of the year—in September, that lovely, golden month, quiet with the ending of summer, when the lush and verdant forests and fields seem to be resting—I get to thinking of another faraway September when we were children down on the old farm.

---

* A tool similar to a pickaxe with a flat blade on one or both sides, used for loosening the soil.

† A foul-smelling gum resin from various Asian plants that was used in folk medicine to repel disease.

One day at the close of school came a message to our teacher that we children—my two brothers and myself—were to be sent up the road to stay at Grandfather's that night. Coming out of a clear sky, we were somewhat bothered about it, but having been brought up to do as were told and not to ask questions, we went.

Came the morning, and back down the road home we came, after Grandfather explained proudly that we had a new little baby sister at our house. A baby sister, I thought. Indeed! Why, I'm the only girl in the family! This just can't be right!

Then my brother Lee, age six, said, "Where, Helen, do babies come from?"

"Well," I said, "I'm not sure, but I've been told that an eagle or stork over in Europe brings 'em. But there's one thing for sure: I'm sure to goodness going to put a stop to it, that's what!"

I took a dim view of the whole matter, wondering why Grandfather had given me a good "dressing down" as he called it, 'bout being "no help to my parents" and being too much of a "tomboy," and racing all over the woods and fields on horseback like a wild Indian with my long curls of "cockle burrs." The three of us went on home only to find out that Aunt Drusilla's children—our cousins, whose mother was helping out—had beaten us to our favorite chestnut trees and chinquapin bushes. Impatient and busy when we asked about the new baby, she ordered us out to the woodpile to bring in chips and stove wood. "You're in the way," she said. "Get on out of here."

It was then the die was cast, so to speak, for there on the chopping block at the woodpile lay, dead, my small pet chicken. Its leg had been broken by my horse stepping on it, and I'd made a splint and bound it up and loved it. Reckoned it had gotten underfoot the night before in the general excitement, and Dad had taken the short way out to get rid of it.

So, getting madder and madder, I said to the boys, "Look, we're leaving here, right now, that's what. And moreover that baby in there they're making such a fuss over is a *girl*, and I've always been the *only* girl in the family, and I'm not going to stay here. No sir, they don't like me anymore, and right now we're leaving. Then they'll be sorry for the way they treated us when they find out we've gone forever."

"But," said my brother, "where will we live? What will we have to eat?"

"Oh," I said, with supreme confidence, "we'll go straight up on Sedgey, out the cattle lane. They can't see us if we go that way, and we can sleep in that Indian wigwam we built out of poles up the mountain on the trail. We'll have wild grapes and chestnuts and chinquapins. We can live 'til we get over the rim of the mountains. Over there there'll be kind people who will be glad to have us."

I went on to explain that we were beautiful children. (Ah, the sublime confidence of youth.) "Oh, we'll be fine," I said. "You'll see!" So away we went, on up the tall, tall mountain that rings our little valley to the north.

The evening shadows were growing ever deeper, the forest was beginning to look more and more formidable, and finding no chestnuts or grapes, thirsty and terribly tired, we sat down to rest, and from our lofty mountain top we looked down on the farm. There was smoke curling from the kitchen chimney, and we knew that Alice, our maid, was starting supper and that there would be hot biscuits and ham and no telling what all for supper. With the hunger that assailed us, we were unable to cope with our independence. And besides, it was getting cold.

So I said, "Maybe we'd better go back home and get an early start tomorrow morning. But you boys just remember, I'm not through with this thing yet. It's just that we got a late start today, and I'm not sure that we've been gone long enough to have taught them a lesson. They just can't shove us around and treat us like we were nobody on account of a little ol' baby girl. I'll bet they'll be awful glad to see us."

When we arrived back at the farm, Aunt Drusilla greeted us happily. "'Land's sake," she said, "you children get on in the house and get a bath and some clean clothes." And as she bustled busily around, she said, "When you get cleaned up you can go in and see your pretty little baby sister. I do declare, you ought to be ashamed of yourselves, off fooling around when you ought to be here helping out."

Hazel Hill, age fifteen, in 1907. The second daughter of Sarah Frost and Frank H. Hill, she married Willett Prevost Sloan. *Courtesy of Robin Phillips.*

I was somewhat taken aback and heard a woeful little wail from the bedroom. "What's that?" I said, and Aunt Drusilla replied, "Why, that's your new baby sister." Before she could finish, I was on my way to the bedroom. I said, "What do you mean letting my little baby sister cry like that?"

And the next thing I knew, I was in my mother's bedroom, and she placed the baby in my arms. While I held her and rocked her in the rocking chair, all the past hours were forgotten. And my baby sister, who has always been the joy of our lives, now is Mrs. W.P. Sloan of Horse Cove.

When the Peddlers Came

That was the time, living our quiet life here, that we children loved. He's gone now, gone with the "horse and buggy days" and the surrey with the fringe around the top, and ox carts and covered wagons. Mother would call us in from play, and the peddler would unroll his wares to our wondering eyes.

There would be Jew's harps—it's been a long time since I've seen one of those—and there'd be little toys that would wind up and do all sorts of flips and turns. And chewing gum and red-and-white penny bars of coconut candy, to say nothing of the Irish linen tablecloths, red-bordered and fringed, and other beautiful linens to tempt Mother. Pins and needles and fancy soaps. Sometimes the weather was bad, and Mother, who was the soul of kindness, would have the peddler stay for the night. Many a tale he'd tell us of the old country sitting by our evening fireside.

And then, sometimes, 'bout once a year, I reckon, there came the piano tuner in his buckboard—a sort of glorified buggy, it was—to tune up and tinker with Mother's Steinway grand, given to her by our great-uncle Gideon Frost at the time of her graduation in 1878 from Quaker College, which he built and endowed at Locust Valley, Long Island, New York.*

It was the first piano to come to the pioneer village of Highlands, and Dad said it took six mules and Mother's six-foot-two brother, Uncle Charley Frost, and four other men to heft it to the mule-drawn wagon from the freight station at Seneca, South Carolina. Three whole days were consumed over roads little better than a trace, fording the treacherous Chattooga River on the way; they had to wait hours for the flooded river to run down low enough to cross. Finally, they landed it home and into the parlor of the Frost homestead here, the summer home now of the Sydney Farnsworths of Memphis.† Dad and the others allowed as how, if another piano ever came to Highlands, they'd be no party to it.

Came the time once, though, when Mother was busy about something, maybe canning vegetables, and the stove repairman, who also sharpened scissors, knives, etc., drove up. Mother, busy and absorbed, answered his inquiry about repairs rather shortly, I reckon. So it was that turning around to drive away, he stopped and called back to Mother, who was on the back porch, "You're a Yankee ain't you?"

Mother answered, "Yes, I am. What of it?"

---

* Now known as the Friends Academy, a Quaker college preparatory school.

† The Hutchinson House, now part of the Old Edwards Inn and Spa at Main and South Fourth Streets in Highlands.

Says he, slapping the reins and starting off, "Don't like 'em. Never did. Fit 'em fer four years up in Virginny, and ain't got no use for 'em yet."

Mother, bless her, who loved the South and was an ardent supporter of the Lost Cause, began laughing and called him back. They had a great time talking while he got out his scissor grinder. Mother found various and sundry odd jobs about the place for him and finally sent him on his way somewhat mollified.

Dad remembered once one of his Horse Cove neighbors coming by his way from Highlands. Drove in with as fine a pair of horses to a double buggy as ever you saw, from way out yonder, 'bout Durham, and he's set up a table there in Dr. O'Farrell's drugstore. And blessed if he hasn't got a lot of tobacco in little white sacks and some little papers, and he's showing the menfolk how to roll up the tobacco inside of them little papers. Sort of licks them together, he does, and calls 'em "cigarettes." Who was that man? No less than the first R.J. Reynolds!

Speaking of the custom of feeding people and their staying overnight, looking backward, I don't see how Mother, who adapted herself so beautifully to a pioneer way of life, ever knew how many would show up with Dad for a meal. So it sort of came about that we girls, in setting the dining table, often

The Hill House, 1888. *From left*: Leonard Hill, Hoyt Hill, Frank "Pa" Hill, Harry Hill, Sarah Frost Hill, and Hazel Hill. *Courtesy of Helen Hill Norris family.*

set an extra place for what Mother said was "the Man in the Woods"—her way of defining an extra guest.

One cold winter day came a Mr. Harshburger from Washington, D.C., who was the post office inspector on his biyearly rounds inspecting the rural post offices of Western North Carolina. When he'd finished going over the records, Mother, being postmaster of the Horse Cove post office at that time, asked him to spend the night. Since it was very cold, about ten above zero, he accepted gladly.

Waxing talkative after one of Mother's wonderful suppers, Mr. Harshburger said, "You know, your hospitality here in the South is amazing. The only time such kindness has been exceeded was a while back when I was late getting to a very isolated little office over in Painter Town, Laurel Country in Transylvania County. When I'd finished going over the records with the gentle old couple who kept the office, Mr. _____ said, 'Stranger, hit's cold and hit's a-spittin' snow outen the North, so you jes' let me put up your horse and feed him and stay with us.'

"Looking around and seeing only the two-room cabin and one bed, I came out with, 'But do you have room for me?' 'Well,' my host says, 'there's a shuck bed,' and that, Mr. Hill," the inspector said, "is what I'd call 'going over and beyond the call of duty' and your termed 'southern hospitality.'

"'Er,' he says, 'you can sleep twixt me and the old woman!!'"

A Wonderful Christmas

This is a true little Christmas story.

It was cold that winter, a long time ago, down in Horse Cove where we lived, so cold that Dad had to chop holes in the thick ice of the creek below the barn for our horses and cattle to drink, and the ice actually froze around their faces on the way back to the barn. It had been snowing off and on for two weeks, and when Christmas Eve morning arrived it was two and a half feet deep and hard on top, so that we children, with our homemade sleds that Dad made, came flying down the long hill back of the house. Into the house we'd come trooping to get warm, then back again to swoosh down the hills.

Because of the snow and ice, no one had been able to get a horse up the steep road to Highlands for Christmas shopping, fixins and presents, and Dad and Mother, looking at four expectant, childish faces, were really worried. Finally, Dad told Mother to give him the Christmas list—that, in some way, he was going to try to go. He saddled up Old Charley, and taking some bags and Mother's list, he rode away, with the wind howling and more snow piling down.

He came back very shortly, with icicles hanging from his mustache. He was leading the horse. It seems that the snow had packed up under Old Charley's feet so that he went lame and couldn't walk.

I was the oldest, and I began to think something had to be done. We sat and sat and looked at one another. Then Mother, with the same courage that had caused her to adapt herself to a frontier life, said, "Look here now, it's Christmas, and we are going to have the finest Christmas ever, don't any of you worry." And then she told Dad to go out and kill two of the fattest hens and to build a big fire in the stove so she could put water on to dress them.

"Hurry now," she said. "We've got to work fast." Then to me she said, "Helen, run over to your uncle's—here's two bags—and tell him to send me as many red apples as you can carry. Then come back and take the other children uphill to coast on your sled. Your father will build a big log fire there for you to warm by. Keep the children up there 'til I get through here."

Later, upon entering the house, we saw that a beautiful tree stood ready in the living room, and a big iron kettle had turned out several platters full of homemade candy. There were two cakes on the long pantry table ready for icing and several mince pies. The house was filled with a spicy, Christmassy fragrance and had definitely taken on the Spirit of Christmas. From somewhere, Mother had come up with some little red candles, which were placed in tin holders on the tree, and two big bowls of snowy popcorn, which were ready to string and drape over the tree. Dad brought in some finely powdered mica dust he'd beaten up, and we sprinkled that over white cotton balls and over the green tree. It looked simply beautiful! Then Mother went to the organ and played some Christmas hymns, and we danced around the tree and sang along with Mother and Dad.

The children were then bathed and put to bed, tired but happy, knowing with the sublime faith of childhood that old Santa Claus would be there in the morning.

Dad came in with two of the cutest little cornstalk fiddles you ever saw for my two little brothers. From the bottom of an old trunk, Mother brought out a small package for me: a book and my great-grandmother's gold breast pin. Dad unlocked his tool chest, bringing out a set of carving knives he'd been hiding away for Mother, then when the four stockings were filled with candy, popcorn balls, and apples, we sat down to rest for a minute. It was midnight.

Suddenly, Mother said, "Helen, that little girl living up under Black Rock Mountain in one of our renting cabins will have no Christmas."

Oh my goodness! We must do something. What did she do? She packed up a good-size box with such things as we could spare, and taking me by the hand, away we went over the snow, a half-mile up the trail so that one little child would find that there really was a Santa Claus next morning.

Sometimes I like to think of it yet when Christmas comes, how two people faced one Christmas with true courage and faith. On the way back from the cabins that night, to keep me from thinking about how cold I was, Mother explained the constellations and stars shining brightly overhead. The Star of Bethlehem shone as brightly in the East as it did 1,900 years ago.

The Little People

And what became of them. I sometimes wonder.

She generally came on a Monday morning to do our washing. Tall, strong, wise—we all loved her. Her name was Esther, but we children for some reason called her "Easter." And because of her "remembers," we knew that if we hung around her long enough, helped with the chunking of the fire under the washpot, and kept the tubs full of the clear, spring-fed gravity water in the yard, we'd get her started telling us about when the folks came over the Wilderness Trail from Pennsylvania in long wagon trains, just like the ones we see now on television.

How I remember that big washpot boiling away out there in the wash house. Looking backward now, I remember Mother's father, Dr. Charles L. Frost, had it shipped down from New England. It held about fifty gallons, I reckon, maybe more, and had been used up in Vermont for boiling down maple syrup. It didn't have any legs, just a rounded bottom. Dad had built a furnace for it to set in.

I remember a second tub full of white clothes soaking, and the colored ones, along with the men's socks and overalls, sorted into another pile, waiting.

Easter, over her first flurry, sort of calmed down, and looked out through the west window up to the Blue Ridge that guards the western rim of the cloistered valley. There used to be strange doings up yonder under "Lover's Leap." Those were the granite cliffs one sees between Playmore, the summer home of the Monroes of New Orleans, and Wolf Ridge, the Ravenel summer home nearer to Fodderstack Mountain.

"What strange doings, Easter?" Oh we were off now with questions.

"Why, haven't you heard about the Little People?" Easter said. She was rubbing away now on the washboard on soiled cuffs and collars. "You've heard and know about how the witches come at night sometimes and plait and braid your horses' manes into stirrups and ride away on a strange trip in the dead of night. And you, Helen, always fussin' how you had to untangle Molly's mane when you ride her to town."

"Yes'm," we chorused. "But what about the Little People, Easter?"

"Well, nobody ever knew where they came from or where they went to, but some folks say they came in here on tiny little mules."

Aha, I thought here to myself. Burros, like the ones out west. And Easter went on, "They wore clothes that had big, bright nail heads across their coats, and they were little and very dark, and nobody could talk to them or understand their talk, either. And for a long time they went around under them cliffs up there and worked at some mines. Don't know if they found anything or not. Doubt it, but they being strange and all, and having such strange ways, reckon most folks sort of let 'em alone. They say there's some of their offspring here yet, or at least some of the old folks say that one or two of 'em went a courtin' and played guitars or banjos and married two of our own folks. When you hear someone say, 'When the Portuguese were here,' that means the 'Little People.' No, they weren't the Indians, just the 'Little People.' Now off with you, and come back in time to help hang out these clothes."

Now I said to my small brothers, "Those little people were Spaniards, and they came here with a man named De Soto, looking for gold. That's what I read about him in books, and moreover, I'll bet a dollar he was down here in the Cove. Let's go over yonder to those old deep pits on the end of Black Rock. No tellin' what we'll find!"

Such is the world of fantasy that dwells in childish minds. However, Mother had warned us to stay away from the old mines, as some of the shafts, sunk in ancient times by some unknown people, were deep and fearsome. I guess they found gold. I know Grandfather Hill did, because when he first came into this unbroken wilderness, he would take his gold down to the towns and trade it for corn. The late frosts were in May and June and the early ones in September. It was impossible for a corn crop to have time between frosts to mature.

Just a few summers back, along the road near the old place came a man digging away on a steep clay bank. "Madam," he says politely, "can you tell me where the gold in Horse Cove is?" Just like that! "Oh, yes," I said, dropping into my native patois, "My Grandpappy, he took it out long time ago."

Speaking of the "Little People," I remember one little Joe who had a shoe shop right back of Mr. Bascom's store. A happy little man he was. Louise Bascom, Mrs. Watson Barrett, and I used to enjoy dropping in to see him when we were children. We watched him trim sole leather into half-soles and put them on shoes with little wooden pegs, Louise solemnly saying that it was fun to hear him talk. Later on, we both came to know when we'd acquired some book learning, that the lingo he spoke was a mixture of Spanish and English. Joe, in speaking of his ancestors, knew only that his grandfather "came from across the great waters."

At any rate, they're gone now, the "Little People." Along with the Indians and pioneers, they have passed into the limbo of the past. And only the forest-clad mountains hold their secret. Those strange days lost in antiquity.

A Little of This and That

I've always maintained a part of the fun of living here is being an individualist.

A few years ago, my sister, Mrs. Hazel Sloan, and I got around to considering selling off a small tract of five acres from the old farm down in Horse Cove up under Black Rock. Sent word or wrote the surveyor, the late Ray Norton, to come down and make the survey. Weeks passed—silence. In town one day, we went into his office to ask why. In his usual quiet way, Ray said, "Well, I'll tell you. You girls ain't got one bit of business selling off that piece of land. It's part of your father's and mother's original home place, and I don't aim to have no part in it!"

We sort of looked across the desk at each other and laughed, Hazel and I. Why, of course Ray was right, and I don't know what ailed us to consider it in the first place. It just goes to show, as I said, a "belonging" that's out of this world—where old friends and neighbors, some of them descendants of our forefathers, look out and are interested in what concerns one another.

Looks as though I'm back from "outside" in plenty of time for our traditional "poke salet." Called up a neighbor the other day. One of the young'uns answered the phone to the effect that "Ma's out hunting salet."

Reminds me of the time, way back, when Mother and the aunts down in Horse Cove made a sort of ritual of going out in the fresh spring air, with the smell of fresh-turned earth over in the back field where the men were ploughing, the air filled with birdsong. There they'd go, armed with a short, sharp knife, their aprons tucked up, looking for lamb's quarter, yellow dock,

Helen Hill Norris, *left*, and her daughter Helen Norris Flippin. *Courtesy of Robin Phillips.*

wild lettuce, and creasy,* while back at the house we were told to keep the pot boiling with a big fat piece of side meat in it, ready for the salet.

"A little sorrel,"† Aunt Ursula would say to Mother, who, coming from New York City and trying her best to become a good mountain pioneer, was a novice. "Sorrel adds a fine taste to wild greens."

Much of the early settlers' pioneer lore came from the Indians, as well as the knowledge of the use of many medicinal roots and herbs. But that's a big subject.

As I said, it's nice, it's wonderful to be home. I didn't really want to go, but the four young Norrises‡ were "out there" waiting for me, and it was wonderful being with them. I ran into several local history events both in Alabama and Tennessee that have never been published. Sort of intrigued me. For instance, Dr. Long in Guntersville, Alabama, and his wife, both archaeologists, took me to the spot on what was the old Tennessee River before the TVA lake system went in where, on the Trail of Tears, the Cherokees had to camp many days while log rafts were being built to get them across the river. And also, I went with Dorothy and Luther Turner§ to Fort Payne, Alabama, where Sequoyah, that wonderful, intelligent Cherokee, lived for several years and wrote the only Indian alphabet that's ever been published.¶

---

* Creasy greens, also known as upland cress or winter cress, are similar to watercress and are considered a southern delicacy.

† A perennial herb whose pungent, sour leaves are used in salads and as flavoring in soups and other dishes.

‡ Helen Hill Norris's children Dorothy, Jack, Helen and Frank.

§ The author's daughter and son-in-law.

¶ Sequoyah (circa 1775–1843) began developing a written language for the Cherokees in 1809, thinking that it would help his people maintain their independence. By 1821, he had come up with a system of eighty-six symbols representing the syllables in the Cherokee language. Its simplicity made it relatively easy to learn, and soon it was being taught to Cherokee children in schools.

On the banks or high escarpment along the old Mississippi River below Memphis, I came to two high Indian mounds. Prowling around with John and Helen Flippin,[*] I found a marker, an iron cross sixteen feet high, proclaiming that the much-maligned De Soto[†] crossed the river on his farewell leave-taking of the eastern states. Doubting this, we went back home looked it up in *Ridpath's History*, and for once the statement was correct. He crossed between the 34th and 36th parallels.

GRANDMA ALLEN'S PHILOSOPHY

Grandma Allen was wise and very old—wise in folkways and the ways of mice and men back yonder in the old days. She hadn't had much "schoolin'," she said, as she swished out her pickle bean barrel and set it out to air in the late August sun.

One thing about us that amuses our northern neighbors is the way we, down here, fall into the habit of calling people we are fond of, regardless of relationship, "Aunt," "Honey," "Uncle," "Grandma," etc. Looks as though they've followed suit for they have Grandma Moses.[‡]

Be that as it may, I'd gone up under the mountain after the cows. The mountain to us children never meant anything but Black Rock, rising over a thousand feet of sheer granite above the level of our old place down in Horse Cove.

I'd generally go for the cows early so I could spend a little time with Grandma Allen and listen to her tales, for Grandma Allen was a woman who remembered.

We sat out on the porch, stringing and snapping the late beans for the pickle barrel, while from the cloistered forest beyond the spring branch there fell on the evening air the liquid notes of the hermit thrush. That songbird, to my mind, has no equal. And to my childish mind, their music converted the deep woodland, with its perfume of rare, late-blooming honeysuckle filling the upland air, and the music of rippling water, into a cathedral. Dad used to go there, I remember, and he'd stop and listen and once he said,

---

[*] The author's daughter and son-in-law.

[†] Hernando De Soto (circa 1496–1542), the Spanish explorer credited with discovering the Mississippi River.

[‡] Anna Mary Robertson Moses (1860–1961), known as Grandma Moses, became one of the most famous painters in the United States when she was in her late seventies, known for her colorful depictions of rural life.

Sally Sloan Phillips, *center*, the author's niece, with her daughter Sally Lee Phillips and Hazel Hill Sloan on the Hill House steps, 1944. *Courtesy of Robin Phillips.*

"There's no man-made church, Helen, that will ever equal it." As I stood in Notre Dame Cathedral in Paris last year, I thought back through the years of his spoken thought.

Well, Grandma and I were busy with the beans. She was saying, "School's beginning. I never had no schoolin' to speak of, and I been studyin' some way to send Tom, that grandson o' mine, off someplace to be educated. Seems like I sure woulda liked to a-been educated. Sam, my old man, never got one bit of school. I remember one day when we took a load of chickens up to Highlands to sell to the hotels and boarding houses. I sent Sam into a place where I saw some folks around, and he came on back to the wagon and got in not sayin' a word."

"'Sam,' I says, 'didn't they want anything we had out here in the wagon?'

"'No,' he says, 'they 'lowed as how they didn't want anything but some poultry.'

"We'd gone on then, turned back down the mountain with our load of chickens headed for home. You see, if Sam had've had schoolin', he'd have known what poultry was.

"Seems like the Allens never had no sense anyway. Allens traipsin' off over the mountain with a banjo under their arms, headed for a frolic or an all-day singin' or some fool thing." Now, *snap, snap* went the beans.

"About Tom, he's not bad lookin', and whether or not he takes to books don't matter too much to me. What I want is for him to learn to put on airs like your pa. Always seemed to me your pa had about the nicest set of airs I ever come across. Moreover, I went to court once down at Franklin during court week, and the likes of them lawyers cavortin' in their swaller-tail coats and billed shirts and gold-collar buttons I never seed before. Doubt if they had much more sense than my Tom, but they'd been off to Raleigh or someplace and learned how to use what they had."

"Maybe so," I meditated, rounding up old Bess and Brindle, and—because she'd been swapped back and forth to Uncle Bud and Bill Toy—a mean cow I'd named Speculation. She was the meanest cow I ever saw. I climbed a tree every time I'd go up to the pasture for the cows 'til after Speculation had passed and gone on down the trail. Maybe Grandma Allen was right about having an education. But about puttin' on airs, now, guess I'd better talk to Mother 'bout that.

HIGHLANDS' FIRST GOLDEN WEDDING

Reckon it was long back in the Gay Nineties sometime that Highlands gave that oyster supper in honor of Dr. and Mrs. H.T. O'Farrell's fiftieth wedding anniversary, and the late Louise Bascom Barratt* and I, young'un-like, got in on it someway. Louise, who later became a writer of prominence, along with the writer of this column, always managed to be in on near 'bout everything around town, playing around the big grounds up at her father's hotel, the Bascom-Louise, now called Lee's Inn,† riding horseback and whatnot. Anyway, came the night of the oyster supper and we were on hand.

Seems transportation of fresh things like oysters—perishable stuff in those days, with no refrigeration or ice—was quite a problem. So ordering about three bushels of fresh Chesapeake Bay oysters, which had to come on the mail wagon all the way from Dillsboro by way of Franklin—delivery on time was a problem, to say the least. Be that as it may, preparations went on blithely. A cooking stove was installed in Boyton Hall‡ (it's the large building just back of Tate's Inn and was Highlands' first town hall), while two long trestle tables knocked together went the whole length of the big room,

---

* Louise Bascom Barratt (1885–1949), who was born in Highlands and kept a summer home there, was a playwright and novelist who contributed to the book for *Artists and Models*, which ran for 519 performances on Broadway in 1924 and 1925.

† Lee's Inn, at the current site of the cottages at the Old Edwards Inn and Spa, burned in 1982.

‡ The corner of Third and Main Streets.

Louise Bascom, *left*, and Helen Hill Norris. *Courtesy of Helen Hill Norris family.*

covered with some of Highlands' expert housewives' finest table linen and decorated with evergreen leucothoe sprays, and green galax. Candlelit and all, it looked quite festive!

Mr. Durgin, whose family came here to make their home from New England in the 1870s, was in charge of the menu and decided on fruit cocktail for the first course. The city fathers bought oranges at a dollar a dozen (some of us can remember when they were that high and considered a luxury).

"Everybody and his dog" was there, folks all dressed in their Sunday clothes, but the mail wagon bringing the oysters still hadn't come. Pappy Durgin, covered with one of Mrs. Durgin's big white aprons and brandishing a big spoon, stoked the wood stove, prancing around and uneasy. Mrs. O'Farrell was in her original wedding dress and orange blossoms, the doctor in his broadcloth cutaway coat and white tie. Everything was OK except that the mail wagon hadn't come with the oysters! They started with the fruit cocktails when Pappy Durgin hollered out, "Go slow, folks; here's Jeff Stewart with the oysters."

Uncle Dave, sitting next to our little schoolteacher, where Louise and I had wedged our way in, got excited, I reckon, and diving into his cupped orange, he splattered juice all over the teacher's new blue silk dress. She let out a woeful wail because, by some freak, and dyes not being what they are now, the blue silk was slowly turning yellow every place the juice hit the silk, much to Uncle Dave's consternation and the little teacher's dismay. By the time Louise and I got over trying to smother our uncomfortable laughter, the spots had turned a bright, wholesome orange, but we helped her best we could, assuring her the spots made the dress prettier than ever and added color. It did!

'Bout that time, in comes the balance of the menu. Never was there such an oyster stew, never so much good-natured fellowship, everyone making a fuss over the heroic mailman, who, after rubbing down his tired horses and feeding them, joined the party. He'd been delayed because of a washed-out bridge at the foot of Cowee Mountain between Dillsboro and Franklin and had near 'bout driven his team too hard to get the oysters here in time. It was a real party, an Old-Time Highlands time, with clever speeches and "Auld Lang Syne" and other popular Gay Nineties songs.

Dr. O'Farrell's drugstore was where Frank Cook's real estate office is now.[*] Quite Irish, as his name would imply, he dispensed castor oil and paregoric with a twinkle in his eye, and it was on the front porch of his drugstore that no less than R.J. Reynolds, the original one of the R.J. Reynolds Tobacco Company of Winston-Salem, sat one day and showed Highlands men how to "roll their own" while peddling his smoking tobacco through the country and driving a pair of horses hitched to a buckboard, a sort of double-seated buggy.

Also, Dr. O'Farrell was one of the first vestrymen in the newly organized Episcopal Church of the Incarnation and organized the church's first choir, and it was always a Friday night custom of the O'Farrells to have choir practice at their pretty home on Fourth Street near where the Crosby home is now.[†]

---

[*] The corner of Fourth and Main Streets.
[†] The corner of Fifth and Spruce Streets.

HORNETS

Came the time these, the meanest of all stinging insects, after careful consideration by the boss hornet, decided to set up housekeeping bang up under the packed eaves of our "little white house," as we children used to call it—being a rural and very necessary structure before the days of inside plumbing and its consequent sanitation.

Someway, we'd become accustomed to the hornet's nest being there and had watched the progress of these architects of nature and the world's first paper manufacturers with childish interest, careful always to be very quiet, as Mother had warned us to be, and not make them mad.

Every summer came a guest, a friend of the family, an Episcopal minister, who oftentimes held services at the Highlands Church of the Incarnation and at the Cashiers Church of the Good Shepherd. During weekdays, Mother got him to coach us in such studies as our small, rather frontier-like school had not provided—such subjects as history, Latin, English literature, etc.

He was a great lover of nature, and there were long walks in forest and field with him while he explained and told us the story of these, the oldest mountains in the world—stories that nature had left folded away in rocks and plant life. Next morning after he came that summer, he proceeded to make his usual call at the little white house, but no one reminded him of the hornets! What took place caused considerable uproar, to put it mildly.

Here he came around back of the garden and on to the woodshed where Dad was stacking stove wood—in a sad state of dishabille, to say the least. He was holding on to such garments as best he could while he slapped at his head and face to brush off the hornets, which had apparently resented an unknown caller and gone into action proper. We kids, as usual, took off in every direction in gales of laughter, with Dad and Mother shaking their heads and making motions at us. Mother ran out with a box of soda, and she and Dad doctored up the Reverend's face, while Mother, in her usual impulsive manner, excited-like, kept saying, "Oh, gracious goodness, let's get soda on the other stings."

"Ah yes, Mrs. Hill," quoth he, "just give me the box of soda that I may repair to the privacy of my room. The attending to my other wounds is a very personal matter."

Since he was to conduct the service at the Episcopal church the next day in Cashiers, we all, admonished by Mother, waited on him hand and foot to

Hill House, *left*, and Captain Day's Cottage in the 1890s. Frank Hill built this little cottage for Captain W.A. Day, a widower and retired railroad mechanic from Virginia. He rented this place and took his meals with the family in the main house until his death in 1928. *Courtesy of Helen Hill Norris family.*

get the swelling down, for we wanted so much to go to church with him. We knew, though, if he didn't get the swelling down and get to looking normal, that when we sat demurely in the pews of the church, we'd giggle out loud. Strange to say, came Sunday morning and our Reverend Hoke, looking more saintly than ever in his white surplice, was OK. We heaved a repentant sigh of relief while he intoned the ever-beautiful morning service in that very lovely and restful Church of the Good Shepherd.

However, he said afterward we should educate the hornets for, he went on to say, they took him at a great disadvantage.

That night about the dark, they ended their brief existence by way of a lighted newspaper at the end of a long pole.

They Flew In—and Walked Out

Guess it was long 'bout the time the flying machine business was in its infancy, and a feller by the name of Charles Lindbergh, little more than a fair-haired boy, flew the Atlantic in what, by comparison now, looked little more than a crate with a motor and two wings.

Long 'bout that time, a couple of young fellers flew a little "cub" plane straight into Horse Cove. They flew straight through the narrow gap on the south, where Big Creek tumbles and foams over many a granite boulder from Colonel Howe's Waterfall, and almost straight into the face of grand old Black Rock, which guards the valley on the north, rising a sheer wall of solid granite a thousand feet high from the valley floor, and upon whose perpendicular face no human foot has ever trod.

Suddenly, confronted with the mountain facing them, the boys promptly "pancaked" their plane, landing bottom side up in the creek that flows through the old farm. There, Dad and Luther, both of them busy in the field, found the plane upside down, the wings resting neatly on either bank.

Dad, bless him, never known to be other than equal to any emergency, and not one of we children ever knowing what his reply would be on any subject under discussion, comes out with, "Hey, fellers," bending over a peek to see if they were unhurt. "Hey, need a little snort of mountain liquor, don't you?"

Well, Luther, who helped out on the farm, took out down to the house and told mother, "Mr. Hill wants a rope," calmly, just like that.

The Hill House farm as seen from the Horse Cove Road overlook, Highlands. *Courtesy of Helen Hill Norris family.*

"Nuthin' the matter, Mrs. Hill," he said. "Just an airplane upside down in the creek up in the big field with two fellers in it."

Up to that time, only one plane had ever flown over the Cove—imagine! So it was that Mother, always priding herself on keeping up with current events, fairly exploded! She took off, calling back to Luther to get the rope out of the tool shed, to "put more wood on the fire," and to "put the coffee pot on."

"Goodness," she said, "a plane down and those poor boys. They'll need food. Tell Leila to get out a ham, Luther."

Well, Dad and the boys and Luther, with the rope, dragged the little plane out into the meadow. Word traveling fast by the grapevine, as there were no telephones, folks began pouring in for a look at the plane—from town, Cashiers, and all around. The road was crowded. A plane in those days, especially in our little sheltered neck o' the woods.

Anyway, Mother and Dad got a big kick out of all the excitement, and folks piled into the Big House for dinners. Why, it was just like the Fourth of July!

An Old Landmark Goes

Some of us sort of hate to see it go, the old Highlands Manor standing proudly through the years in its broad acres back from the Horse Cove Road.

In the course of time, change, and progress comes the time for it to go, though, and before long the old manor will be sold with its furnishings and the building dismantled.

How well I remember Grandfather telling me of the days when our proud little resort town was only a broad forested savanna, used then only for cattle grazing by one of the Dobsons of the Cartoogechaye valley near Franklin. I believe it was Mr. Ben Dobson's father who built what I know was the first house in Highlands. It was a double log cabin with a "dog-trot" between the two rooms, and it stood right where the Highlands Manor now stands.* Hughey and Mary Ann Gibson lived there for some years, tenants of the Dobsons, to look after and care for their large herd of cattle.

The country was wild then, and stock on the range had to be looked after against marauding Indians and wolves and bears. The New Englanders, coming in close behind the opening of Highlands by our founding fathers,

---

* Near the corner of Sixth and Chestnut Streets.

Kelsey and Hutchison, often spoke in terms of strong affection for Hughey and Mary Ann Gibson, and I've often wondered where they were buried, for they were Highlands' first and only residents for many years.

Later on, in the late 1870s, came my maternal grandfather, Dr. Charles L. Frost of New York, looking for a place to retire from his practice. He bought from Messrs. Kelsey and Hutchinson (Mr. Hutchinson later founded the city of Hutchinson, Kansas) the tract of land now occupied by the manor, the Farnsworth home, the Episcopal church, the Hudson Library, the west boundary that runs along the street on which the Catholic church now stands, the Presbyterian manse, and many other attractive homes, clear back to where the old Durgin Sanitarium was and eastward toward the Ravenel Lake. I don't recall the exact acreage, but I reckon property was mighty cheap then, and guess Grandfather didn't want to be "hemmed in."

Anyway, seems he was greatly intrigued by the beginnings of a house Mr. Hutchinson had started building for himself on the gently sloping hill where the old home stands now, the summer residence of Mr. Sidney Farnsworth of Memphis, adjoining the manor property. It's interesting to note in passing that this English manor–type home has for its sturdy foundation huge oak timbers, cut and split lengthwise and set up on solid stone footings. The logs were cut right on the spot, for Highlands was heavily forested then.

Did you ever see the cross section of a large hemlock tree, now exhibited at the Highland Museum,[*] which was cut out of the forest when Main Street was opened? It was an old tree when Columbus discovered America, I'm told, counted by the rings.

Some years later, grandfather decided to sell the place to Mr. T.G. Hall of Charleston, South Carolina, who went over to the site of Hughey and Mary Anne's cabin, near the spring, and built a new Dutch Colonial home that now forms the west wing of the manor. It is where this writer spent her childhood.

It contained—amazingly, among other things—Highlands' first bathroom. That was before modern plumbing appliances, but Grandfather, obdurate and enterprising, with the help of H.M. Bascom's metal shop, managed it somehow, everything built of zinc and copper—tub, lavatory, etc.

Among other things, Grandfather—who was accustomed while living in New York to watching the incoming shipments from foreign countries for treasures—had picked up two beautiful white marble carved mantelpieces

---

* The Highlands Biological Station, Nature Center and Botanical Garden.

Dr. Charles L. Frost's home, the Hutchinson House, now owned by the Old Edwards Inn. *Courtesy of Robin Phillips.*

from Italy that were used in the parlor of the new house and in the dining rooms overlooking the clear, beautiful lake. These, I'm sorry to say, were lost when a later owner decided to put in modern mantels, and the priceless marble ones were broken to pieces when removed.

The warm, rich tones of the imported wall-to-wall carpet—how I remember the frantic housecleaning every spring when they were taken up, sunned, and beaten out on the clotheslines. Don't you know they would have loved our modern vacuum cleaners!

Some way, through the passing of the years, the tall, carved Italian alabaster vases that stood gracing the base of the Florentine mirrors and the imported carpets are gone now, and the once-loved fields and gardens and orchards, the lake with its colorful crowds of ice skaters—where I used to watch the men with the big saws cut up great blocks of ice for storing away in a sawdust-filled icehouse to be used in the summertime.

Those were happy days for me and for a man who came to love the soil, loved people, and was loved by all who knew him: my grandfather Charles L. Frost.

HIGHLANDS' RECORDS

The return of spring with all its mountain charms—flowering woodlands and forest-filled birdsong, the little town, preening itself from a frozen and "holed-in" winter, the likes of which even the oldsters fail to remember in the annals of the long-distant past—finds everyone happily going their way armed with garden tools, paintbrushes, etc., and going about under a welcome and beneficent sun with hammer and tongs. For it is cleanup and green-up time in the Highlands.

Kind of makes me think of how, back in May 1883, the little town of Highlands was incorporated. Then came, quietly, the beginning of what the founders of Highlands little realized—the beginning of what John Parris* recently referred to in his column about Highlands being "the most popular and richest mountain resort" in this section of the country.

Grandfather Hill,† Highlands' first mayor, left some interesting and amusing records, now stored in the town's vaults for safekeeping. The town was incorporated on May 7, 1883. Seems the first town meeting was held that month at Grandfather's home on Main Street, which is the quaint house on Horse Cove Road later owned by the late Talbert Staub of Geneva, Switzerland, and now the home of Mr. and Mrs. Lewis Rice.

Grandfather had won the election for mayor by six votes over his opponent, John J. Smith, who came to Highlands in the late 1870s along with many others from New England. At this meeting, they elected the town's first commissioners. They were as follows: H.M. Bascom, C.B. Edwards, and Alfred Morgan. Oath of office was given under Mr. I.M. Skinner, a newcomer from Boston, with Alfred Morgan, secretary, and H.M. Bascom, treasurer. Among votes cast and passed at this meeting are some rather amusing ones, fitted to the times and a way of life now gone.

First, it was against the law to bring in and sell intoxicating liquors.

Second, all livery stables were to be cleaned daily and refuse removed.

Third, stray cattle and hogs were outlawed on the streets inside the town limits, and a fine of five dollars each was to be imposed and paid by owners of same. They were to be held or incarcerated "without bond or benefit of clergy," I reckon, until said fine was paid, half of the fine going to the town and the other half to the persons or informers who found the stock roving the streets and turned in the name of the owner.

---

* A native of Sylva, North Carolina, John Parris was a London-based correspondent for the United Press and the Associated Press during World War II. From 1955 until 1997, he wrote the "Roaming the Mountains" column for the *Asheville Citizen-Times*.

† Stanhope W. Hill was elected Highlands' first mayor in 1883.

Frank H. Hill at
the beach in 1940.
*Courtesy of Helen Hill
Norris family.*

Off the record, though, information came about the village grapevine
that the plan didn't last long, because some schoolboys with a head for
business baited several droves of hogs into town by scattering corn along
the mountain roads and trails, thereby collecting their $2.50 part of
the fine. Of course, this caused some irate stock owners to take the law
into their own hands and march into town with their rifles across their
shoulders, armed with axes to knock down the "pound" (a pen made of
stout boards over there across from where the old schoolhouse is being torn
down) and turn their hogs and cattle loose, driving them right through
town in broad daylight. And being "kin" to most of the city fathers, believe
me, nothing was said.

In 1886, another record says that due to the fact that an overnight guest of the calaboose* had tried to burn the place down after being tried and released, the board voted to increase the pay of the night watchman to ten cents an hour.

WHAT DID THEY THINK?

There's the time a few years back, down at the old place in Horse Cove, my dad getting a little tired at ninety years of age, decided he must have an outdoor lounging place for his after-dinner siesta. Looking about, I remembered a folding cot or day bed at my summer home just up the road a little way.

I decided to bring it on down, then looked around again and finding no one around to furnish transportation decided it would be fun to travel real native style. With the help of one or two of my neighbors' kids, we caught up old Kate, an old worn-out, lop-eared mule left over from farming days over in the pasture. We rigged her into a harness of sorts and found an old flat wooden sled on runners in the wagon shed. With the children from roundabout—we gathered up more as we went along, some piled up on the sled and others running alongside, and almost all the hound dogs in the valley bringing up the rear—away we went.

I'd grabbed up an old battered straw hat that had seen better days, and all in all, with me walking alongside driving old Kate, we looked like a movie group staged for pictures. I was getting one big kick out of it, and the kids and dogs were in high feather too! We felt highly independent and proud of our ability to go after things on our own way.

Then along came a big car of summer tourists from "outside." They drew up roadside for my "entourage" to pass, for we had to have room, the sled being old and worn and "side-goddlin'," you see. Never has it been my lot to see such concealed amusement as I saw on the faces of those car occupants. Oh, we were the "Real McCoys," an "outsider's" idea of what was typical of the old-time southern Appalachians' product.

The young'uns, cute little blonds of every size, barefoot and wide-eyed, stared wonderingly as I brought Old Kate to a halt. We looked at the "city slickers," and I, proud of my ability to drop into the local patois, says, "Howdy"—on an impulse of mischief, I reckon, and knowing I didn't stand a chance with the situation, as it was, establishing myself as a person other than what I appeared to be: a person who seemed to be a poor woman with

---

* The town jail.

Sally Sloan Phillips with her daughter Sally Lee Phillips outside Hill House. *Courtesy of Robin Phillips.*

a passel o' children and dogs and an old mule, maybe hauling wood, who'd never been beyond the rim of her mountain valley.

So it was that I couldn't resist following a conversation like this:

One woman in the car, with an indulgent, benevolent smile and manner, said, "You live around here?"

I broke a twig from a bush by the roadside, using it for a toothbrush to make like I was a snuff dipper, and then answered laconically, "Live down the road apiece."

The woman took the bait and ventured another question: "Oh, and are all these your children with you?"

"Not strictly speakin'," I said. "Some of 'em air my grand-young'uns and some of 'em jes' 'yard chillun' live aroun' here. I sort of gathered 'em up, you might say, as I come up the road. You see, my pappy, he's down with his back sort of, and I aim to go up here and get him an old army cot fer to rest on daytimes."

Then someone in the car said, "What do you do for a living, my good woman?"

Keeping my face straight I 'lows, "Raise taters, pick berries, and the old man, he sells a little 'mean likker,' sometimes trades 'coon dogs,' and one thing an' another."

About that time, one of their party comes out with what I was watching for—a camera. Deciding my hoax had gone far enough, I took off my old straw hat, straightened up a bit, and in what I considered my best "Oxford accent," and pleasantest and most gracious manner, wished them "bon voyage."

"Please excuse me," I said, "I'm in somewhat of a hurry."

I left them staring after me and my picturesque outfit as we proceeded up the road, with Old Kate's one limp ear hanging over her one good eye and the sled, the mule, and the dogs—the old wooden sled still running sideways, with me walking alongside and thinking how much more fun it is in this old world to be underrated instead of overrated.

ROCK HOUNDS, THEN AND NOW

Time was, way back yonder, the pioneering gold miners passed by the gems that are now creating so much interest in this and surrounding North Carolina counties.

These were the early "prospectors" and miners. They were looking for gold and found it, not in large quantities nor in nuggets, but fine placer gold, washed from the gravel in the clear mountain streams that tumble with such sparkling beauty through rock-ribbed ravines and over waterfalls into the rivers below. It was no uncommon sight then to see an outfit along the road, a wise and kindly man leading his pack mule with pick and shovel and gold pan strapped to the saddle along with his grubstake.

When the first settlers came, Grandfather said the season for growing foodstuff, such as corn and oats, etc., was too short for crops to mature between the late spring and early fall frosts. The valleys down below being highly productive, it became the custom of the few who braved this life in our surrounded frontier to go to mining for gold, which was taken to Augusta, Georgia, to be weighed and sold, and the money used to load up the covered wagons with supplies.

There is the "gold branch" down Horse Cove way, still showing in its piles of gravel and debris along the stream the "diggings" of over one hundred years ago. High up on the ridge alongside are two large, almost bottomless open shafts, or pits, where the "paydirt" was hauled up by a windlass and buckets to be washed in the branch below.

Along these "dumps," and even along the roadside where there were gullies, one often came on beautiful clusters of amethysts, richly purple in color, with as many as fifty faceted, clear gems in one cluster. It was no uncommon sight then to find these used as doorstops or lying out in the yard somewhere, so plentiful they were.

And there was Garnet Hill on the old Whiteside Cove Road, now long gone back to the forest, so full of garnets that the buggy wheels used to start them rolling in little shoals. Of course, they were not all good ones, but once every so often among so many, a clear, good one would turn up. Reckon there's no telling how many semiprecious stones were lost or thrown away as useless back when the country was new, for always they hunted for gold.

The Cherokees' name for gold was *dahlonega*, for which the gold fields in North Georgia were named. The meaning in the Cherokee language is "yellow metal," and that's what that rascally Spaniard De Soto was searching for when he passed through the mountains with his five hundred Indian burden-bearers, who later, because of his cruel treatment, led him into defeat and away from Dahlonega and the "yellow metal" he coveted. That, however, is another story, and among my notes there is some authentic, unpublished data on De Soto that I'll get into some sort of form for this column later, I hope.

Well, the gold that was in these here hills has long since gone, I reckon. It was mostly in small deposits, or "pockets," and has given way to the more exciting business of gem hunting. But it was a rather romantic era, and possibly the California Gold Rush took a large percent of the miners away.

Speaking of the Gold Rush in California, in which I had a great-uncle and maternal grandfather from New York, reminds me that while we were in California back in '38, coming out of Santa Maria, here comes what looked like a movie set—an old man leading a tough-looking little burro, a pick and shovel and gold pan and grub all tied on. I got the folks to stop the car and got out to talk to him. I was sort of scared to barge in on his quiet dignity, but he was real friendly and just a real old-time gold prospector—not a part of a movie set at all, as I'd been afraid he was.

He gave me a picture of his "outfit." He said he was on his way to the John Day River Country for gold and added quite casually that he was "just out of jail"!

Somewhat taken aback, I asked him what he was in jail for.

"Oh," says he, "I was just in for a little while. The 'jedge' cleared me. Killed a feller. Shot him. Didn't mean to kill him, though. Nice sort of feller, too."

About this time, I began looking around to see how close I was to our station wagon and my boys.

Willet Provost Sloan, *seated in uniform at right*, and friends from Clemson College. *Courtesy of Robin Phillips.*

"You see," he went on, "I just aimed at his foot and he started his car as I shot, and it killed him. Nice feller, and I hated it, but he took pictures of me and my outfit after I'd told him not to, and the reason the 'jedge' cleared me is because California forbids pictures being made without a state permit, especially of things that are historical."

With that, and with a polite bow, he proceeded calmly on his way to the John Day River Country with his picturesque outfit for more adventure. I just hope he made no more "killing" mistakes!

WHEN THE RAIDERS CAME

Sometimes, riding through the beautiful sheltered valleys and the little hidden coves with their clear, spring-fed tumbling streams, one cannot visualize them ever being other than what they appear: quiet and even restful. However, right after the Civil War—or the War Between the States, rather—the infamous Kirk from Tennessee* led his band of three hundred desperados, formed from renegades from both the North and the South,

---

* During the Civil War, George Washington Kirk (1837–1905) commanded the Third North Carolina Mounted Infantry, a Union regiment known as "Kirk's Raiders." The regiment embarked on a series of raids in the mountains of Western North Carolina, seizing and destroying the property of Confederate supporters, who regarded them scornfully as renegades.

straight through here in search of blood and loot, for he killed on sight any man or men who stood in his way.

He ranged through Cashiers, Whiteside Cove, Horse Cove, and Glenville, all through the counties of Jackson and Macon.

He came one winter's night to the home of the late Judge Felix Alley's father in Whiteside Cove. Colonel John H. Alley had been commissioned by Zebulon Vance to serve on the Home Guard* because of lameness resulting from several years' service in the Mexican-American War. He was at home, all of his family sick with measles, when suddenly the front yard was filled with horses and men. They surrounded the house and called for Colonel Alley to come out, saying that they were out to destroy all men serving on the Home Guard. But Colonel Alley, undaunted and composed, asked, "Is Kirk your leader with you?" When told that he was, he asked for Kirk to come in, alone.

Rather disdainfully, I reckon, Colonel Alley looked the bandit over, although he himself wasn't armed. He remembered that the home of my Grandfather Hill, his old friend, had been raided a week before (that was the old home down in Horse Cove), and he remembered the bandit and his gang taking my grandmother's saddle horse from her on the wagon road to Highlands and leaving her to walk home, frightened and alone, down the mountain road after dark.

Oh, and the old colonel was smoldering mad. That he was in danger of losing his life at the point of the pistol aimed at him as he sat propped up with pillows on his bed mattered not at all. His scornful gaze looked Kirk over quietly.

"Well, Colonel Alley, you're one of the ones on our list; but tell me, just what do you think of me?" queried Kirk. (Grandfather said Kirk was a very vain, glamorous sort of fellow.)

"Now you know, Kirk," Colonel Alley replied, "there's not enough words in the English language to give you any idea of what I think of you. You're about the sorriest specimen of humanity I've ever laid eyes on."

With that, Kirk fired his pistol at the Colonel, but it didn't fire. He snapped it five times and still it didn't fire. "I'll get you," Kirk yelled, reloading.

Then one of the gang looking in through the door rushed in, knocked the pistol from Kirk's hand, drew two long-barreled ones from his belt, and shouted, "This is my colonel, and he saved my life once when I fought the

---

* In 1863, under Governor Zebulon B. Vance, the North Carolina General Assembly created the Home Guard as an emergency police force to round up deserters, skirmish with Union forces, and maintain order. White men between eighteen and fifty were conscripted. By the end of the war, there were eight regiments comprising about twelve thousand men.

Mexicans with him. Sure as God made little apples, I'll kill the first man that makes a motion toward his gun."

Well, that didn't end it, though. They raided the house; took every bit of clothing, shoes, blankets, and all the food they could find; shot three milk cows; and stole the Colonel's black saddle horse that had been his pride in the Mexican-American War.

They went on over the hill and killed Mr. Ned Norton, Colonel Alley's brother-in-law, who had just returned from the Confederate Army in Virginia, but that's another story. I often pass by the remains of the old Norton home where this happened—just a small pile of stones where the cabin stood—but that's still another story. Maybe I'll get around to telling it one of these days.

Anyhow, in that quaint little well-kept Norton cemetery—on the left as one drives from Horse Cove to Cashiers—lies the body of the man who saved Colonel Alley's life. Two days after the raid, Colonel Alley found his body not far from his home.

"They'd shot him for defending me," said the Colonel, "so I made his casket with my own hands and buried him best I could in my own family plot.

"It was the best I could do," the Colonel said, as he bent over to place his small hand on the curly head of a small girl who used to love to sit and listen to tales of long ago.

CABIN FEVER AND "SPLASH DAMS"

With all the rain this past week, being shut in and all, I got tired of reading, tired of Scrabble playing, even a little tired of TV and the World Series, and near 'bout broke out with cabin fever like Wild Bill Hickok of the Wild West days.

So it was, come Saturday afternoon, I took off with friends to meander down the lovely mist-hung trail, walking with raincoats over our heads at Dry Falls. What a sight! Foaming, dashing, as we gazed upward, just as a faint ray of sunlight struck the falling waters. It was like looking through a delicate veil while the roaring sounded and resounded like organ music against ages-old canyoned walls. Looking down on the gorge through the golden lace of leaning birch and fitful sunlight, I wished that everyone could see it and that the postcard people had some colored shots of that scene. Now, a few hours later, the glory is gone.

Secret Falls in Horse Cove. *Courtesy of Robin Phillips.*

Standing there, I fell to thinking of the old-time timbermen who came, way back yonder, into the Virginia forests, and the way they had of making use of the rivers to carry their logs to the lowlands and mills. They used to build barriers along the river, especially the upper branches of the Chattooga called "splash dams," cutting their logs and sledding

77

them down the steep sides of the gorge into the river. Then when they had enough logs, and the river was high, they'd knock the shims loose, and *whoosh!* Away and gone were the logs, quick and easy transportation.

I think the idea originated up in Maine among the early lumbermen. Wasn't a bad idea, but somewhat dangerous for the lumberjacks, because sometimes the logs "acted up" and got jammed and had to be straightened out. Seems that happened one time to a local lumber crew, and Joey Canter, the one with the long red beard almost to his waist, volunteered to go in and get the logs untangled. Moving out over the roaring sluice—dangerous business anyway, out in the middle of the river, logs upending and churning about fast—Joey lost his footing, and in a few minutes one couldn't tell Joey from the logs, only the long red beard floating 'round and 'round in a sort of whirlpool. The other men jumped in to help him, and finally one of them yelled out, "Fellers, he's going down. He's going down sure as h-ll! Some of you grab him by his beard and pull 'im out!"

About that time, Joey made one final effort and pulled up on the bank, shaking all over, and shaking the water from his beard as he gasped out, "Heard you fellers talking that foolishment about grabbing me by the beard. I'm ordinarily fond of my beard, and I was afraid you'd tear 'em loose pullin' me out, so I knew if I wanted to save 'em I'd have to get out somehow. You see, my grandpappy and my pop both wore beards like these 'til they lay a corpse, and I aim to wear mine 'til I die."

"Oh, shut up, you old fool," says Tom Griffin. "I near about drowned myself gettin' you out. If that's all the sense you got, wish I'd let you go down the river, beards, logs, and all."

Speaking of our beloved surrounding frontier, I fell to wondering how much longer we can keep it to ourselves—a selfish sort of way of thinking, though, come to think of it. Be that as it may, here comes the October 10 issue of the *Saturday Evening Post* with the whole front cover picturing a rich, rolling valley at Boone in Western North Carolina in Watauga County. Artist John Clymer is to be congratulated.

Wolfpack: 1885

Reckon the present generation has another definition for 'em, but last winter when our Never Never Land was a mess for weeks on end of snow and ice, we Highlanders were, for the time being, "isolationists," weather-speaking, meeting it with a solid and somewhat humorous attitude, with a dash of cabin fever from being housebound. There came to mind another winter back in the '80s, so the old folks said, and the old thermometer stayed at a steady reading of seven below zero to fifteen above nearly all winter long.

Moreover, a deep ice-crusted snow covered the mountains, hills, and valleys, so it was hard times, I reckon, for the bears and wolves that roamed far and wide foraging for food. Grandfather was away (seems he was forever off on horseback somewhere or other, for it seems, according to Grandmother, he had no other idea than that he was a lawyer, doctor, and judge of the universe in general, carrying his medical books and law books in his saddle bags). Grandma was making out pretty well with the wood stored with kindling in the little shed room off the back porch, and plenty of food.

Along about ten o'clock one night, the dogs kept scratching and whining at the door to be let inside (a thing that rather mystified Grandmother), excellent watchdogs and utterly fearless as they were. She finally opened the door and let the dogs in, *then* she heard them! Came a chorus from the mountain rising high above the house and barns. She slammed the door shut hurriedly and stood thinking a bit, for what Grandmother heard when she stepped out on the porch was a wolfpack on the hunt. She had heard them once before as a child back in Rutherford County.

She wasn't afraid for herself and her babies, she said, but there out in the barn lot was the stock. With the absolutely brave and quiet fortitude that has from time out characterized the pioneer woman, she wrapped up—axe in one hand, gun in the other—and out she went. There at the barn lot, after driving the young colt, the cows, and calves into the stables, she proceeded to nail tight the heavy crossbars across the doors.

Closer and closer down the steep, snow-covered mountain toward the orchard and vineyard came the pack. And moreover, across the valley on Rich Mountain came the call of another wolfpack, evidently coming straight across to join forces. Oh, they were organized, no doubt of that. Naturalists say there is no animal known that has the hunting wisdom of a wolf. Now both packs were closing in, one on either side of a little pioneer home unprotected but for a brave little stout-hearted woman who, with the strongest-known emotion on earth, was going to protect her home and her babies.

Back to the house then she went to nail down windows, pull shutters tight, fasten door latches, and build up a blazing fire. Taking down and loading the shotgun and rifle, she was ready for them. Then she remembered the

Black Rock Mountain in Horse Cove. *Courtesy of Robin Phillips.*

sow with her pigs and the sheep in the low broad shelter, wide open to attack. Out again she went, this time carrying her gun across her back so as to leave her arms free. By now the wolves were circling the wood lot just above the barns.

Throwing such rocks and timbers as she could lift, she weighted down the low roof over the log pens, nailed the doors shut, and turned to run. Then she saw, standing at the open edge of the forest, the leader of the wolfpack, snarling. She fired the shotgun, both barrels, square at his head and, of course, being frightened, missed her shot, but she dashed on into the house and to safety.

Then, before long, she heard men's voices outside. Her gunshot had been heard by two neighbors who were out trying to save their own stock from the ravaging wolfpack. So what with letting out a Rebel yell or two remembered from Civil War days and what with a drink or two of mountain dew under their belts and the firing of guns in which Grandma joined, they sent the two packs high-tailing back into "the Divide," a connecting and almost impenetrable fastness between Black Rock Mountain to the lower reaches of Whiteside Mountain.

But that is the last known account of wolves in packs in our part of the Appalachians. In fact, except maybe for a few heavily timbered portions of states bordering Canada, they've just about disappeared from the American scene.

Mountain Mysteries

A silent sort of day, overcast, autumn-tinged, and rather pleasant. We came to Judaculla Rock, that strange one covered with signs, symbols of a bygone race. Who were they, the ones who left them there? Well, one wonders.

It lies in a cow pasture, on a little slope where Caney Fork winds its way through a pleasant valley to the Tuckasegee River. One leaves the highway to Sylva on the left, up a hardtop road to a sign pointing right, and on over bridged Caney Fork and down a little rain-washed trail to find the huge granite boulder slanting toward the creek, covered all over with symbols and signs, worn down somewhat, how many years no one knows, by winter snows and freezes and the passage of time.

Archaeologists and scientists alike have been puzzled for generations by the carvings of a turtle, a symbol in some ancient archives of long life, and in the Spanish legend it has been claimed that the drawing of a turtle indicates hidden treasure. There are seven distinct chiseled markings or lines drawn from the bottom to the top of the rock, sort of fan-shaped, spreading out wider at the top. And on the lower left-hand side there is a huge seven-fingered crude outstretched hand. I wonder if this number seven has meaning, since there are seven long lines, with seven fingers (I sort of figured out seven branches on the tree of life).

The entire surface has small round holes, pretty evenly spaced and rather shallow. Couldn't figure out if they were man-made or water-worn holes. After thinking it over, I sort of think they were made by the ancient sculptor. Well, guess no one will ever know, for as far back as the pioneer settlers questioned the Cherokees, there has been no knowledge about its origin. The only saying is that "it's always been there."

There is also the legend of the existence of a mythical giant that lived on the mountain above the rock named Judaculla. Purely an Indian superstition, I suppose, but as the years, decades, centuries pass and the mystery of the strange markings on Judaculla Rock remains, with the streams and its mountains guarding the secret, I wonder.

Not being anything of an archaeologist, can't help being intrigued with a rock found years ago on our old farm in Horse Cove. It's approximately seventeen inches long, twelve inches wide, and nine inches thick—a reddish, very hard substance, closely resembling the skull of a prehistoric giant lizard. There's the flattened under-jaw and irregular bone structure brow. There are small indentations that look like brain cell cavities, one large, round eye socket, going back farther than can be probed with a ruler, about an inch and a half in diameter and resembling fossils seen in some museums. It's funny that in these, the oldest mountains in the world, there's no record of prehistoric life preserved in them anywhere.

Last year, in a small stream bed near Mirror Lake, I came across a flat stone of the same substance as the head—a reddish, hard-as-nails stone, with small, clearly marked animal tracks plainly indented in it. Over beyond Toxaway, to the right of Highway 64 in an isolated area called the Canebrake, a surveyor told me a few days ago that coming out on top of a granite-capped "bald," there were barefoot tracks of a man of a huge size. Well, that's "one for the birds"—can't explain any of it. Maybe someone can.

What with naturalist Dr. L.S.B. Leakey's report to the Pan-African Congress on Prehistory of the discovery in the Belgian Congo of a skull that is supposedly 600,000 years old[*]—a human skull, reassembled by experts at the Coryndon Museum[†]—there's just no telling what in time, and with the aid of science, may at some time be unearthed and explained in our own Mysterious Mountains.

---

[*] In September 1959, Dr. Louis Leakey, the paleoanthropologist and archaeologist, presented at the Pan-African Congress on Prehistory in Leopoldville, Belgian Congo, the discovery at Olduvai Gorge in Tanzania of a hominid skull that he initially estimated to be 600,000 to 1 million years old. The skull was discovered by Leakey's wife, Mary, and was later found to be about 1.75 million years old.

[†] Leakey was the curator of the Coryndon Memorial Museum in Nairobi, Kenya, from 1945 to 1961. It is now part of the National Museums of Kenya.

MOUNTAIN HOSPITALITY

Looking backward to the early days of the Model T Ford. You remember, don't you?

The gas tank was under the front seat, with a gas gauge that looked like a ruler that you used ever so often to see if you had any gas. This necessitated removing the front seat, of course. And a spark-plug wrench, for about every fifty miles, the spark plugs got fouled with oil and had to be taken out and cleaned, else you would be running on one cylinder or two, which meant the old Ford was bucking like a wild bronco.

And the collapsible bucket was a very essential part of operations, for when you came to hills to climb, the radiator would boil the water out. This meant you stopped at every branch to give that thirsty radiator a drink. And a flat tire was something else! No demountable wheels in those days. You had to pry the tire off the wheel with two tire tools that always came with the toolkit, being careful not to pinch the inner tube. You then had to patch the hole in the inner tube with a cold patch (later you could actually put on a hot patch by applying a match to the gadget). Then came the laborious task of getting the tire back on the wheels, but that wasn't anything compared to pumping up the tire, especially on a hot day and on the side of either a *dusty* or a *muddy* road. It had to be one or the other. But let's don't throw off too much on the "Tin Lizzie," for their advent just about revolutionized our way of living. Here is my story.

In those early days of the Model T, some friends from Augusta decided to drive to the mountains for some fishing at the old Grimshaw place in Whiteside Cove. And believe it or not, they bragged much on making the trip up with the unbelievable average of twenty miles per hour. Get this straight: it was not twenty miles per gallon they were bragging about, but twenty miles an hour. This is understandable, for those were horse-and-buggy days.

After some good fishing (and fishing was good in them thar days), these friends left for home. Down around Mountain Rest, South Carolina, the old Ford conked out. A Native, riding a horse with a sack of meal for a saddle, ambled by, brought the encouraging news that a man living a "piece down the road" was a sort-of mechanic and might help them out of their difficulty. This kindly stranger promised to send the man up to see what he could do.

In about an hour, the "mechanic" came in a "rattle-trap" car. After much punching and probing, he said he knew what the trouble was but would have to go to Walhalla for a repair part. So he pulled our friends and their

Whiteside Cove Summer Chapel, originally a schoolhouse, built by the Nortons and the Whiteside Cove community along with Frank Hill around 1918. *Courtesy of Robin Phillips.*

Frank H. Hill and Sarah Frost Hill. *Courtesy of Robin Phillips.*

Ford down to his house, arriving pretty close to sundown, and he lit out for Walhalla. Rather forlornly, our friends sat on the porch of a dilapidated mountain house to await developments.

Soon, their spirits were revived by the odor of country ham frying and coffee boiling. Full hospitality was extended. While they were eating a sure-enough good supper, the mechanic "host" arrived with the necessary part for the Ford. Two lanterns were swung from the limbs of a tree, and as our friends went to sleep (their first experience with a shuck mattress), the sounds of hammering came from the old Ford that was undergoing emergency "night surgery." Awakened finally by the smell of coffee and country ham, our friends partook of another good meal at breakfast time and were thrilled to hear that the Ford was ready to go.

But a difficult situation soon arose. In asking for the price for services rendered, our mountain mechanic scratched his head and repeatedly came up with the answer, "I just don't know how to charge you." Our friends repeatedly stated, "We thank you for your kindness and want to pay." After much hemming and hawing, the mountain fellow finally blurted out, "Would three dollars be too much?" Yes, TIMES DO CHANGE!

DOES A MOLE HAVE TEETH?

This little rodent, the plague of local gardeners, was once the cause of an argument that lasted for days between our two old uncles down home in Horse Cove.

But speaking of ground moles and their destructive inroads through the soft black earth of our gardens, there came a day when one of the neighbors, exasperated and somewhat defeated, proceeded to write to headquarters—the Agriculture Department in Washington—for instruction on the subject. He received the following instructions on a government-printed form:

"Select a cloudy day, and using a pitchfork, one should stand well poised over the mole runs, which are indicated by broken earth. Upon movement of the broken earth, proceed to hastily pierce the ground with the fork, thereby annihilating said rodent."

Quoth the dirt farmer, "Now who in tarnation has the time to play polo with a pitchfork and a ground mole?!"

Getting back to the uncles and their argument as to whether a ground mole has teeth or not, one uncle took the stand that the mole had no teeth at all, but made his road underground with strong front feet in search of grubs, for they are carnivorous. He went on to say that the small ground mice cleverly followed behind through the underground tunnels, destroying bulbs and plant roots as they fed on them, to which Dad and Mother agreed.

But still the unconvinced other uncle, glowering and twitching his eyebrows, held to his original statement to the effect that the ground mole did it all. With both uncles getting madder and madder, their argument continued on through several dinner-table discussions. It finally ended by Uncle Buck's setting his mole trap and catching a mole, then working additional hours to catch the marauding ground mouse. He then proceeded to carefully expose the head structure of each and, of all things, took hammer and tacks and nailed them to Uncle Charlie's bedroom door! Not a word was said, for by this time the two old dears weren't on speaking terms, having reached, I s'pose, the point of no return.

However, after a few days' silence, they fell into another argument concerning the origin of the tune of "My Country, 'Tis of Thee," bursting into song during dinner and pounding home their respective points on the table 'til all the dishes shook. One contended that the song was composed by an American writer; the other said it was adapted to the anthem from England, "God Save the King."

Uncle Buck won again, by dear Mother's taking the two old coots into the little Victorian shut-off parlor, getting out her history of music, opening the piano and playing both the American and English versions, which were the same. And so another argument was settled.

Election Day

Now that our mountain winter has passed and the signs of spring are all around—a freshly turned garden plot here and there, with bright-eyed robins following along in the wake of the plow looking for worms, and the upland pastures greening up with young lambs frisking about while their mothers feed on the sweet new grass—one sometimes gets a little impatient waiting for reluctant spring to come shyly tripping in over our high country, and we take off in high feather on minor excursions for the "lower towns," as the Indians used to call them.

To quote one charming Thomasville, Georgia, lady who, residentially speaking, has become "winterized" and is a welcome addition to our growing winter colony: "Let's get off the mountain." And then it's away and off; picking up a friend or two on the way, we head for the lower levels along the flower-clad slopes along with the ever-beautiful Cullasaja, Tuckasegee, and Chattooga Rivers.

Came a day down at Franklin, seems as though everybody was mighty friendly. There was a lot of handshaking, and folks were all sort dressed and taking a great interest in your welfare, etc. Unusual, I thinks to myself. Then I remembered: it's election month, and that's always a stirring time in Macon County.

Of course, our county seat folks have always appreciated Highlanders and all that, and the two towns have always, since the county was organized in 1828, shared a comfortable sort of rural companionship. I sensed along Main Street a real surge of alertness among the shoppers and my friends.

Speaking of Election Day, 'minds me of something I ran onto not long ago in Alabama, during the last presidential election. I'd gone on an errand to a small country store with my hostess and found the store full of local voters. To my utter amazement, the voters were writing their votes on any slip of paper handy, and two women in charge of the precinct were putting the votes into paper grocery sacks! Now that's the living truth.

Helen Hill Norris, *left*, with her daughter Dorothy Norris Turner and her sister, Hazel Hill Sloan, outside Hill House, 1943. *Courtesy of Robin Phillips.*

I went over and looked at the row of bags setting on the floor, one row marked "R" for Republicans, the other "D" for Democrats. So, curious, I allows, "These votes, what becomes of them?"

"Oh," the lady in charge says, "I'll take the bags full of votes over to the courthouse tonight and they'll be counted."

"And then," I said, "by whom?"

"Oh!" she says, "most anybody happens to be 'round."

How on earth, I thought lamentably, can any section of our supposedly well-organized nation tolerate such woeful neglect and carelessness in as important a thing as an election?

And that reminds me that this Saturday, April 21, the books will be open at the town hall all day and on following Saturdays through May 12. This is highly important in that the election officials wish to make it clear that previous registration does not count and that in order to vote in all forthcoming elections, voters' names must be registered in the new books.

While down in Alabama, speaking about that paper bag voting, I ran across an old-timer and fell to talking to him, he allowing as how he'd been defeated time and again in Marshall County elections. Quite a wit he was, and before I left, he handed me an account of his candidacy for a county office, all written out as follows:

"Failed to plant a crop of peanuts and potatoes and lost four weeks and twenty days out to canvassing. Lost 360 hours of sleep trying to think of how to defeat my opponent.

"Donated one beef and four shoats and five sheep to a county barbecue. Gave away two pairs of suspenders, five print dresses and fourteen baby rattlers. Kissed 126 babies, all of 'em over 16. Kindled fourteen kitchen stove fires, put back up eleven stoves and the pipes that fell down. Carried fourteen buckets of water uphill from springs, walked several hundred miles, lost count of how many lies I told, went to twenty-six religious meetings, baptized four times by immersion, twice by sprinkling, gave nine cents to foreign missions, made love to nine grass widows, got dog bit ten times, and then got beat!"

A Man and His Dog

I know now why the mountain-born keep and love their hound dogs. Some way I've always wondered about that, but not anymore. Not after what happened last summer, I haven't. Protection, that's why. Protection from time out of mind against the wild and predatory animals that once roamed unmolested through this rock-ribbed and unbroken frontier.

Came a night last summer, we were up real late, with card tables up and two games going, while I kept a worried eye kitchen-ward, where I had a pork roast baking. Doors were all open, and that aroma of the cooking roast was sort of overpowering, with all my young crowd making threats toward a midnight feast.

All at once I heard the seldom-heard but definite scream of a panther way up the old road toward the mountain. Afraid to frighten my children, who were already a little panic-stricken and were sort of running around in circles, I explained that it was possibly a dog and hurried out back to close the doors. Then I heard it again, this time right in the backyard. I remembered the old hunter's saying that, oftentimes out on a hunt, they'd never cook fresh meat on a campfire at night because of the danger of its scent bringing in, as they said, "a big cat."

So I proceeded to close up things as tightly as I could—and then how I wished for a good old faithful hound dog!

I'd heard the scream of a panther twice as a child, once when I was late coming home from hunting some sheep ranging on the mountain above the old place, and once again on a cold winter's night when we were late getting in from a neighborhood party and were at the barn putting up and feeding the horses.

We found the unmistakable tracks out in the freshly rained-on sand the next morning. There were the soft, big, padded front-foot tracks and the smaller, pointed ones of the big cat's hind feet where it had jumped from a bank several places up the wood road.

So now I know why the mountain boys keep their dogs. Mighty comfortable thing to have around, a dog is.

FIRST SUNDAY SCHOOL, 1876

Long ago—eighty-four years ago—a little group of people established Highlands' first Sunday school. It was on a Sunday morning, on March 12, 1876, at ten o'clock, that twenty-six persons assembled at what was known as the Log Law House, bent earnestly on establishing a Sunday school. I am of the opinion that the Log Law House was built by Highlands pioneers where the Helen's Barn property is now.* (It was used for a while as a sort of "meeting house" for all matters pertaining to the frontier town. Maybe sort of like the still existing town meeting houses in rural New England.)

According to my information, which I am sure is correct, as careful minutes have been kept and preserved, S.T. Kelsey, one of the two founders of Highlands, was called to the chair, with T. Baxter White as secretary of the meeting. Motion was made and carried that the name be known as the Highlands Union Sunday School, motion being made by Mrs. Baxter White. Motion made by Mr. Arthur Hutchinson, the town's other founder, that it be made a permanent organization. Motion carried. Mr. White was named superintendent, Mrs. Kelsey secretary and librarian, and James Sopher chorister, chosen by the group from different parts of town. Mrs. George Jacobs, Miss Mary E. Wright, Miss Temperance Hill, C.N. Jenks, J.W. Wilson, Jonathan Ford, and Felix Grundy Hill were chosen as the board of directors. The teachers were Mrs. George Jacobs, infant class; Mrs. Kelsey, in charge of all the attendants who could not read; and Grundy Hill, adult class for women.

---

* From 1935 until her death in 1959, Helen Cabe Wright hosted popular square dances at Helen's Barn, which was set back from Main Street at First Street. Square dances at Helen's Barn remained a popular summer fixture in Highlands until 1984, when the property was sold to make way for the Wright Square shopping center.

In a footnote found later, I was rather touched and a little amused to find that Miss Temperance Hill, bent on the preservation of a tiny little organ that the Sunday school group bought, was accustomed to promptly, after the service was over each Sunday, "hist" the organ on the back of the buggy she was driving and carry it home for safekeeping there at the quaint Staub cottage. (Now the home of Mr. and Mrs. Lewis Rice, it was built in 1873 by my grandfather S.W. Hill, who moved from Horse Cove to Highlands in order to help the founders establish and found the brave little beginnings of the village. He was Highlands' first elected mayor, and his carefully kept records of the happenings in those days are carefully preserved to this day in the vault of the town office, as mentioned in an earlier column.)

Stanhope Walker Hill (1815–1894), the first elected mayor of Highlands. *Courtesy of Helen Hill Norris family.*

Those must have been troublesome days, for recorded is the story of invading men, sometimes as many as fifty strong, from a nearby Georgia mountain county who, resenting the law and order being enforced against the sale of liquor in the town, came riding in, armed. No scene now shown on television in the "shootin' up westerns" can in my mind quite equal those early days. There they came, shooting as they rode in on galloping horses, shooting out "window lights," yelling like Indians. But that is another story to be told sometime later, and the way they were finally subdued forms a somewhat tragic and brave tale. Anyway, that's one reason my Aunt Temperance, who later became Mrs. Nathan McKinney, carried the Sunday school's precious little organ every Sunday on the back of her buggy from the Log Law House, lest the Log Law House be burned.

A little touching, too, that Highlands' present Hudson Free Library had its beginnings in a humble little log house by the side of the road. For in the records, it is noted, Mrs. Kelsey was mentioned as librarian, and books were collected and sent as a nucleus for the library by no less a person than Edward Everett Hale[*] of Boston.

---

[*] Edward Everett Hale (1822–1909) was a clergyman and author, best known for the short story "The Man Without a Country."

Nature Notes

Winter in the offing, etc. Watching the gray squirrels and smart little brown chipmunks storing hickory nuts and acorns busily, I came around to thinking on the ways of the provident and thrifty manner in which nature gives them the instinct to prepare for the long winter days ahead.

Long time ago, when I was a little girl, Dad and I were walking through the woods, and Dad was telling me stories of the wildlife surrounding our home in Horse Cove.

"Most everything stores food for the winter except a possum," he said. "That's the doggonedest no-'count one of 'em all.

"One day," he went on, "I was hunting up my wild hogs over around the Gold Mine branch end of Black Rock and sat down to rest by a deep pool. It was real cold, late in January, and small patches of snow around. Here came an old gray possum walking unsteadily down the trail, paying me no attention at all, which I thought rather strange, and also strange that he'd be out in January, away from his den. Well, that old weak, tired, and hungry fellow circled the pool a time or two right before my eyes, then he jumped in and held his head under the water 'til he drowned. He just committed suicide, sure as anything. He's even planned it, too. Of course he may have been the victim of a frustrated love affair! But I reckon he was just old and hungry and figured he'd end it all."

From left: Hazel Hill Sloan, Helen Hill Norris, and Vivian Norris, the author's daughter-in-law. *Courtesy of Robin Phillips.*

ROMANCE

Spring being here, comes a time, according to the poets, when "a young man's fancy turns to thoughts of love." So here is a real local love story.

Down in the Horse Cove valley, there's an old sycamore tree by the roadside—the only one that's known of in the whole area—and it marks the site of an ancient Indian campground that was in use around the 1840s, when my grandfather was commissioned by the government to round up the Cherokees and remove them to the reservation over in the Smokies.

Seems the chief of the Eastern branch of the tribe was named Walking Stick, for whom Walking Stick Road in the Cove was named, and the sycamore tree came to be there because the chief often walked all the way over from Nikwasi, on the Little Tennessee, where our county seat of Franklin is now, and he always carried a sycamore walking stick. On one occasion, at a tribal council meeting at the camp, he left his walking stick stuck in the ground, and there it took root and grew. And standing there today, after 120 years, majestically sharing its spreading branches with the birds and squirrels, is a huge sycamore.

Some years ago, a pair of young lovers was strolling by the tree, and the young man, being very much in love, said, "I wish I had a ring, Mary. We'd get engaged right this minute."

To which Mary replied shyly, "Yes, darling, and it may be that the fairies will leave a ring here for us, because where we are there's a legend about making a wish and having it come true."

With a stick she had in her hand, she was prodding the ground the way people do sometimes when they are talking. Turning over a rather heavy flat stone, she picked up, of all things, a plain gold ring. It was dark with age and caked over with the clay in which it had lain through the years, but when it was rubbed and cleaned, the young lovers realized that their wish had indeed come true. It was a lovely wedding ring.

During the marriage ceremony some months later, it was indeed with the greatest reverence and meaning that Bill said the timeless words as he placed the ring on Mary's finger: "With this ring do I thee wed."

They have lived happily ever since and are one of Highlands' most interesting couples.

WAS THE MOUNTAIN A CHALLENGE?

Often one asks a mountain climber, "Why do you climb it?" The answer nearly always is, "Well, guess it's because it's there!"

Standing 4,460 feet above sea level and facing southward, Black Rock Mountain, back of our old place down in Horse Cove, raises its head and perpendicular granite cliffs on which, supposedly, no human has ever trod. It stands, sentinel-like, presenting a height of over 1,000 feet from the valley floor.

An ages-old mountain whose lofty top once served for smoke signals from one Indian tribe to another, it looked down on the peaceful pine-pole lodges of the Cherokees, grazing their ponies on the acres of lush, tall grass that formed an immense pastureland, long after the lake, a natural formation, had broken its barrier through solid granite to the south and gone.

The mountain, through the passing of time, has seen the white settlers moving in with their covered wagons, my ancestors among them; the passing of nature's children, the Cherokees; and often long and bitter fighting over the grazing land with the white settlers from the south. Primitive battles were fought between the two factions, so old Mr. Nicholson told us. It was not unusual, now and then, years ago, to come across an Indian grave, lovely and stone-covered, on a high ridge in the forest.

Then, too, in the early 1860s, the mountain saw two patriotic young men in their early teens march away to fight with Lee in Virginia for a cause that, in their love for their homeland, was just, and a war that the British have often referred to as the "last war fought between gentlemen."

On a bright, sunny morning back around 1884, three young boys, relatives of ours, despite dire predictions and warnings from the oldsters, decided they could climb Black Rock. The late Hugh Graham Thompson, son of Bishop Thompson of Jackson, Mississippi, also an adventurous spirit, joined them. When the timber line stopped and the solid granite wall to the top faced them, "foot and finger holds" were only time-winnowed, shallow crevices.

Some years ago, one of my family showed me the route they took, slightly east of the center, saying it was by far the most treacherous route they could have taken. Guess it was, for about halfway up (and how they made it that far is amazing), the younger one, Tom Hill, scared to death, with fingers and toes bleeding from cuts on the rocks, yelled to Ted and Graham above him that he aimed to drop! Guess he 'lowed it was easier to die than to go on. The other two decided the only thing to do was to give

Black Rock Mountain in Horse Cove. *Courtesy of Helen Hill Norris family.*

him a good "cussin' out" and make him real mad, and maybe he'd hold on in order to get up to where they had a better toehold on a bigger crevice. Guess it worked, because Dad, when telling me about it years afterward, said Tom yelled, "If I live to get you, I'll beat the stuffin' out of you for calling me a coward."

Folks watching below (for of course a crowd had gathered), knowing the boys were in trouble, had rushed home for ropes and were already climbing up the wooded slope of the eastern exposure to the top, where they tied the ropes to the trees to anchor them and that way dropped the ends over the cliffs and down to the three boys, pulling them up to safety hand over hand. Three pretty badly bruised and scared boys.

Well, reckon it was the same old mountain climbers' urge to "climb it because it's there," for it was only in May 1953 that the highest peak in all the world was conquered. That was Mount Everest in the Himalayas in Asia, scaled by two intrepid members of a British expedition, Edmund P. Hillary and Tenzing Norgay. Mount Everest! Think of it! More than six times as high as our spectacular Whiteside Mountain.

LAW GROUND AND REAGEL'S GAP

When one drives down Highway 28, on many a winding turn of the road one passes, a few miles out going to Walhalla, South Carolina, the old Georgia state "law ground," located in that far-flung Rabun County region, one of the largest of Georgia's many counties, and a large portion of it still remote. The "law ground" now lies unnoticed by passing tourists and visitors, long since becoming abandoned with the coming of good roads and the consequent motorized age with its quick transportation.

Seems that in pioneering days, Rabun County's seat being in Clayton and reached only by one muddy and rocky road from this, the Pine Mountain section, the residents petitioned the legislature to create or set under state law a certain area where legal meetings could be held and civil cases tried by the local magistrate. So it was that on the first Monday in every month for many years, a picturesque group of men with their long rifles gathered not only for local trials but also for a day of "yarn swapping" and trading in general. There were simple split-log benches, a few of which were still there a few years back, and for a while a crude shelter stood there.

The magistrate's records of those distant times are both amusing and pathetic. There's the time a man was on trial for making up his corn crop into a liquid, still familiar, called "moonshine." The judge asked the man, upon going on the stand in his own defense, if he wished to make a statement.

"Yes, sir, your honor," he said, "I sure to goodness do. I live over on yon side of the mountain in the poorest land that ever was, and I've been twice married and both my wives are dead, and left me undoubtedly two of the meanest mother-in-laws a man ever 'cussed' with. Then there's twelve children, all under fifteen years old—two separate sets of 'em, and them all fightin' with each other. And the two old grandmothers, they don't get along, either. So I jus' naturally, judge, have to take to the woods, fire up the old still and 'thump keg,' light my pipe while the pot boils, and study things over. I know it's wrong to make 'corn likker,' but it's the only way I can get hold of any money and have any peace."

The record says the judge reached for his book and wrote, "Silas So-and-So's case tried and dismissed."

Legal notices were posted on trees, and many a local swain and his sweetheart were married in the leafy bower beside the murmuring streams—and many an argument was settled out of court. It's a picturesque spot, a tumbling mountain stream on the left of the highway, laurel- and rhododendron-sheltered. Then, where the stream crosses the road beyond the old "law ground," is Reagel's Gap, named for a U.S. revenue officer by that name who was shot and killed from ambush by a resentful manufacturer of "corn likker." Dad said that a man with him, who was an old friend named Cole, from Jackson County, was also fired upon but escaped by horseback, only losing his hat as he dashed up through the short road into Horse Cove and Grandfather's home for help.

Grandfather had one old trusty slave who stayed on after Reconstruction named Dan, and so he and Grandfather drove a wagon down to the gap in the night and brought Mr. Reagel's body to Cashiers. I don't remember if he was buried there or not, but I guess he was. Anyhow, the man who killed him was never known. Dan is buried in the Hill family plot in the Horse Cove community.

He Tried Anything

There was a time once, long before these days of outer space exploration and jet planes, that men, standing earthbound and watching the soaring aloft of birds, longed to be able to fly just like them. Reckon, thinking about this sometimes, it could have been this elemental urge that finally brought about the conquest of the air.

"Looks easy," thought the mountain-born and adventuresome Billy Cook from over in Jackson County, as he stood on the top of old Whiteside Mountain one day and watched those rare birds, the ravens, who nest in the mountain's high and remote granite cliffs—watched their graceful, poised flight out over the forest-clad valleys below.

Being a man of action, he believed he could do it, he told his wife, Varina—a practical woman she was, very dubious of anything or any new ideas. Be that as it may, though, came a March morning with a high easterly wind, and Bill proceeded, with the help of the young'uns—Varina, her nose in the air, 'lowing she'd have no part of such a fool undertaking—to take wild turkey wings from the fireboard that Varina used to sweep the hearth with. He bound them right up snug and tight under his shoulder blades with a groundhog skin string he'd been curing and getting ready for a long time and wrapped 'em 'round his body.

"I'd been eating light for two weeks," he said, "so I wouldn't weigh too much."

Then, taking the big blue umbrella from the barn—kept to "hist" over them when they drove the wagon to town—up the ladder he went, to the

Helen Hill Norris with her son Frank Norris. *Courtesy of Robin Phillips.*

top peak of the roof. He tried several flaps with the wings and looked down at Varina and the young'uns and the neighbors who were making bets on the experiment.

There was a strong wind at his back. Everything was all set.

"Now then, Varina," he said, "in case I fly off so far I can't get back, you and the young'uns'll have to do the best you can. But I'll be back if I don't get too far off, 'cause this thing might take me plumb to the Tennessee line. Remember to kill hogs on the dark of the moon so the meat won't be tough with not enough grease to fry itself. Keep a flint rock in the fireplace to keep the hawks off the chickens."

And with various and sundry admonitions, Bill raised the blue umbrella and took off.

It was some days later that Varina, coming to wash for Grandmother, soliloquized as follows:

"Law me, often we'd bed him down with camphor and Japanese oil and gave him a few drinks of corn liquor and he came to. He says, 'Varina,' he says, 'did I break any bones?'

"'No you didn't,' I says, 'but undoubtedly you're the biggest fool in the state of North Carolina and I reckon now you've learned your lesson.'

"Well," she went on as she punched the fire up around the big washpot full of boiling clothes, "you know what that outlandish old fool said? 'No, Varina, you being a woman and all, ain't got sense enough to know that I can and will still fly like a bird. Next time I aim to rig me up a turkey tail and a pole that will whirl around in the wind and carry me plumb off back of beyond.'"

But after all, who knows? Could have been that Bill's ambition to fly, primitive as it was, was man's first idea of air conquest.

FORDING IT IN 1918

To save my life, I just can't help looking *forward* instead of backward at times like these. Watching clouds overhead, drifting in silent turmoil northwestward over Bill Cabin Ridge, wondering if we're in for more bad weather and hoping for a soft, warm southern wind, bringing warmth and a slow, soft rain, which would wash away our six weeks' accumulation of ice and snow.

Officially it's spring, but nary a sign of it here do we see, and we still live under an all-time record of emergency. Speaking of emergencies, reminds me of the time my brother Hoyt, down in Horse Cove, turns up with an old beat-up Ford—of ancient vintage, even then. Grinning and a little pompous, he announced that we were all to remember he was the first in the family to own a car, adding that he didn't know for sure if he could drive it or not!

We were urged to go for a ride, and piling in, we took off "over the hills and far away," at the wonderful speed of ten or fifteen miles an hour. Came dark, saying we had to get back home and help mother with supper. "Turn around," we said. "Oh," he allows, "I can't turn this thing around. Don't know how."

On and on we went until we ran out of gas, then Hoyt walked back for miles until he came to a country store we'd passed with a gas pump. He returned after a long while in high spirits. We went on again until we came to an old logging road, circled it, and were back on the main road again headed for home. All of a sudden, the brakes gave out! We made it to the store again where he'd bought the gas.

The storekeeper, out back tinkering with his own old car, upon being told about the brakes, proceeded to lay aside his wrench and went into the store, picked up a butcher knife, and hauled out a big slab of side meat. He cut off some big slices of the rind—still no comment, nothing said. He goes out, takes off the wheels, cleans out the burned brake lining, slaps in the bacon rind, neatly relining the inside rim. Still no comment; he just held out his hand for a quarter.

Months afterward, when my brother took his old rattletrap to a service station in Walhalla, the mechanic, taking off the wheels, said, "What in the name of sense is this brake lining in here?" And Hoyt says, "Meat skin. It's been there for six months. Did fine."

Going down to Walhalla shopping one summer's day with Hoyt in the old Ford, the brakes gave way again. He got out, took his axe into the woods, came back dragging a pretty good-size log. He chained it to the back wheels and away we went, bumpity-bump, the log serving fine to hold the car back and reduce the speed. Guess no one can match the mountain-born for resourcefulness in an emergency.

WEDDING "OBJECTIONS"—YES!

Seems as though some of the oddest, funniest things can happen 'round here, and maybe, along with me, one of my readers has wondered sometimes what would happen if some feller "spoke up" during a wedding ceremony and raised "objection."

Comes to mind a fireside story down at the old place when as a little girl I used to beg to sit up late and listen to grown folks talk when visitors came. That night after supper (it was before folks got around to calling the evening meal "dinner"), we'd gathered 'round the big fireplace in the east living room. Our hired girl, Lielia, whom we all adored and who disdained being referred to as a "maid," was with us, and a big pitcher of cider was on the table. While chestnuts roasted on the coals, the folks got around to talking about John Wayman and Dora Boman's wedding over Shortoff way. Seems one of the boys around town, falling in with the idea of the wedding, etc., took off for Franklin and the courthouse to buy the wedding license— on horseback, of course.

The town folks, all knowing the bride and groom, and it being a pretty Saturday afternoon, took off for the Shortoff schoolhouse, which at that time was used for church, too. By the time Smith Allison got back from Franklin with the license, an awful big crowd had gathered, and the preacher wisely decided they'd just have the whole thing outdoors in the open field back of the schoolhouse.

Guess it was a pretty enough scene, with the forest background and the distant rim of the mountain blue on the horizon, and the pretty young bride in a white dress coming across the open field carrying flowers, and with her, the groom. Following them were the mother, father, uncles, aunts, and cousins. It must have been very beautiful in its simplicity.

Be that as it may, proceeding with the ceremony, the preacher came to the part of the service containing the admonition: "If any man here present can show just cause why this man and this woman should not be lawfully joined together, let him speak now or forever hereafter hold his peace."

"Well, sir," believe it or not, went on Uncle Zeb Alley, who was telling the story, "up spoke Zeb Fraley from way up in the branches of a dead chestnut tree, where he'd climbed for a better view, I reckon. Yes, up he spoke real loud. 'I object,' he says.

"A dead silence followed. The preacher, somewhat bothered, replied, 'And why do you object?'

"'Just object,' says Zeb. Dead silence again.

"The preacher, getting pretty mad by that time, came out with: 'You ain't no Zaccheus hiding up in a sycamore tree like the Bible says. You just come on down out o' that tree and state your objection, or some of us 'round here are goin' to work you over.'

"Well, Zeb came on down out of the tree, saying: 'Well, you see, it's this way. According to the almanac, it's the wrong time of the year to get married. And furthermore, the sign of the zodiac on the front page of the almanac shows it's the wrong time of the month. And also, preacher, Smith Allison, who rode plumb to Franklin for the marriage license and paid $1.50 out of his own pocket for it, ain't been paid back yet, so I don't aim to lower my objection 'til the hat's passed and the money made up to pay Allison back. And while that's being done, let's make up enough money to pay the preacher, folks.'"

Helen Hill Norris with her son Frank Norris. *Courtesy of Robin Phillips.*

And so with that, the ceremony was finished, after the collection had been taken up, with everybody happy and wishing the bride and groom a long and happy life.

Yes, some funny things happened 'round here back in those days, but John and Dora did have a long and happy life—right here in Highlands!

OAK TREES AND THE WHISKEY WAR

Once, not too long ago, one of the trees left after the first ones were cut on Main Street in Highlands was a great spreading oak tree that stood right in front of Highlands Inn. An old picture shows children playing in its shade, but it's gone now, to make room for so-called progress.

Since the old oak figured in Highlands' early history, one feels a little sad that it was not preserved. But guess that with the coming of cars and trucks and the passing of the gentle, unhurried days of the ox cart and horse-and-buggy times, there was no room left for the old tree.

Sort of makes me think about oak trees, though, and the part they played in our nation's early days. There's the Charter Oak at Hartford, Connecticut. It went down in a storm in 1856. It once held in its hollowed heart the charter of the New England colonies while we, as a nation, were still under British rule.

Nearer home is the Boundary Tree at Cherokee. Some claim this to be an oak, but I'm of the opinion that it was a poplar tree. Anyway, now the land around it has been commercialized so that there's the Boundary Tree Motor Court, Coffee Shop, Craftsman's Shop, etc. But time was, so an old Indian told me at the reservation, that a sturdy pioneer by the name of Felix Walker obtained a state grant for upward of four miles of land. Looking it up, I find that it was State Grant No. 501, year of 1798. He owned all up and down the Oconaluftee River and Raven's Fork. Quite a man was Felix, for he in later years represented both Haywood and Buncombe Counties at different times* and was with Daniel Boone when he opened the romantic Wilderness Road into Kentucky in 1775.

Walker's homeplace was on Jonathan Creek near Maggie Valley, North Carolina, in the national park, and has been or will be marked by the North Carolina Historical Commission. The Boundary Tree marked the land between the white man's settlement and the Cherokee lands.

Then down in Athens, Georgia, there's the big live oak tree, which is said to be the only tree in the world that "owns itself"—left so that it's never to be owned by the city or any person. And who, reading Sidney Lanier's† "Song of the Chattahoochee," with its musical rhythm, can fail to remember the live oak tree still standing down near the Georgia coast at Brunswick and dedicated to the South's immortal poet.

But back to the Highlands oak. My dad surely had a wonderful memory, else this little book wouldn't be so full of the old days. And how I bless the long winter evenings when as a child around the fire, with a big pot of chestnuts boiling away and Mother coming in with a big pitcher of apple cider, we'd all get Dad in a talking mood and telling us things that happened long ago.

One day, passing a big oak stump near our barn lot down in Horse Cove, Dad said, "Wish to goodness I hadn't cut that tree down. Let's go on up to the pasture under Black Rock and hunt that old fool cow Brindle. She's gone and hidden her young calf in the woods."

---

* Felix Walker (1753–1828) served three terms in the House of Representatives, from 1817 to 1823. During the debate over the Missouri Compromise in 1820, Walker rose to deliver a rambling speech as the House was preparing to vote. When several members tried to cut him off, Walker declared that he was "speaking to Buncombe." A new word, *bunkum* (or *bunk*), was born, meaning talk that is empty, insincere or merely for effect.

† Sidney Lanier (1842–1881) was a musician and poet whose poem "The Song of the Chattahoochee" was published in 1877. He is said to have found inspiration at the foot of an old oak tree in Brunswick, Georgia, that is now known as "Lanier's Oak."

Came night and storytelling time. "About the oak tree, Dad," we young'uns prodded. "You promised."

"Well, about that now. One of the best friends we Hills ever had, Clifford Morris, in fear of his life back yonder during Highlands' Whiskey War, spent many a night in that tree. He was armed and ready to shoot on sight the man or men who sent him a letter after the three days' battle that they were coming to kill him.

"Morris was a dead shot, though, and had come to the mountain from his home in the North for his wife's health." (He had bought the old place long before my family owned it and made an attractive home of the pioneer log house of five rooms, built in 1842.)

"So it was, when things broke loose in Highlands," Dad went on, "your uncles, grandfather, and myself, together with the Alley boys over in Whiteside Cove, all went armed to the teeth to help Highlands out. You see, the law officers of the new town had outlawed the traffic in moonshine liquor brought in from Georgia—long 'bout 1875 that was—and the outlaws were getting busy with threats and shooting up the town on Saturday nights. Last time was a showdown.

"The Georgia men barricaded themselves inside the main hotel with that big tree in front of it. Old Cliff Morris proceeded to climb up in the treetop. He stayed there 'til he spotted a man in an upstairs window and killed him dead as Hector. After that, things subsided somewhat, but the dead man's friends, as time went on, organized themselves into something resembling a real mountain feud.

"And so it was, with danger always lurking in the woods, that we persuaded the Morrises to go back to their home in the North. However, many a night your Uncle Buck and I would keep watch along with Cliff at the old tree I've cut down. And if that old oak in front of the hotel in town could talk, it could sure tell some tales."

Note: If one cares to follow up the story of Highlands' "Whiskey Rebellion," see Judge Felix E. Alley's book *Random Thoughts and Musings of a Mountaineer*, printed in 1941, pages 273–90. It was published by the Rowan Printing Company of Salisbury, North Carolina.

However, when the author came to present my dad with an autographed first edition, Dad said, "Wasn't Tom Fard killed that renegade from the hotel oak, Felix, it was Cliff Morris. I was there and ought to know. And besides, you were just a tad runnin' around in knee-britches."

Harry Hill, son of Frank and Sarah Frost Hill, circa 1920. *Courtesy of Robin Phillips.*

SOUNDS OF A SUMMER NIGHT

The mountains have a lovely lingering twilight, and the sunsets that precede the darkening evening are often varied and colorful, sometimes followed by a golden pink afterglow that's almost indescribable.

Then comes the night, and with it the little wild things of the forest come out of hiding, foraging for food and drink. The sharp crack of a twig underfoot, the rolling of a pebble even, is probably old Bre'r Fox or a bobcat. Funny thing, though, about foxes and wildcats, they don't get along together at all. No sir! They tell me when the foxes began to increase here so fast, the wildcats took off, and time was that young lambs and pigs had to be fastened up securely at night, and chickens weren't at all comfortable on their roosts because of the wildcats. 'Course now, what with Charlie Potts* (our fox-huntin' mayor) and the Edwards' fox hounds, it seems the wildcats have taken off in high-dudgeon and things are sort of under control, but foxes are "foxy." You can't catch one in a trap no matter how cleverly set. 'Bout the only way to outwit a fox is to set a "dead-fall" in his trail to drinking water, but generally speaking, Bre'r Fox passes disdainfully on the other side of the trail.

One sits still and listens. It's about eight o'clock, and clear and haunting comes the call of a whippoorwill from over the hill, the last sleepy note of a catbird or robin from a sheltered tree, and from over on Rich Mountain comes the hoot of an owl. Funny about these owls, for ever since there's any "remembering," they've always stayed right on that one mountain, and no one has ever heard them on any of the other five mountains that surround our little valley. They range from the northern limit of trees in the Arctic south to the Strait of Magellan.

Then there's the hum of a "junebug," a cricket's continuous cheerful note, a soft fluttering of wings way up in the chimney where a chimney swift has built her nest. Later on, there'll be the echoing song of the katydids, and some folks say, "There's the katydid; just six more weeks now 'til the first frost."

But these are peaceful days now to what went on, so the old folks said, for back in those days doors were to be fastened tightly at night, barn doors and sheep and pens stoutly fastened, for those were the days when wolves, bears, and panthers preyed on livestock, and children were warned by their parents to stay close together in groups on their way to and from the district school, and when no man was hardly seen without his gun.

---

* Charles C. Potts served as mayor of Highlands from 1959 to 1961.

Sally Sloan Phillips. *Courtesy of Robin Phillips.*

Guess life back then had its hazards, but it was fundamental, and a survival of the fittest—a way of life that's given way to a modern and a more gracious way of living. However, it's sort of an interesting epic still, with the sounds of a summer night, when darkness descends and lies gently over the ages-old tall mountains wrapped in silent slumber.

THE FRENCHMAN

He came walking in one winter's day down home from "beyond," thinly clad and seemingly a bit shy. Be that as it may, and those being the days when a stranger was warmly welcomed and treated as an honored guest until proven otherwise, the folks weren't long in recognizing him as a French-Canadian named Louis Quesnel.

The fascinating way that he told stories held us spellbound. He told tales about the great northwest mounted police and of nights spent trapping for furs in the wilds of Saskatchewan, all in his quaint French-Canadian patois, or, as we say, "broken English." He bought a small fifteen-acre farm adjoining our old place, and there followed for us many years of strong, proven friendship.

There wasn't much the Frenchman didn't know, from doctoring an ailing cow to advice on medical care for sick folks, and even his advice on points of law was often helpful. It finally came about that, in an emergency of any kind, it became the custom to say, "Send for the Frenchman."

Among the wonderful fruits and vegetables he grew on his pretty terraced hillside garden were a variety of sweet and luscious melons that were started early under small cloth-covered cold frames.

It came about that one early fall—seems as though it was September—Dad and Mother, following their usual custom, took off in a flurry for "court week" in Franklin, where they would visit the Norman Barnards for a few days. No sooner had they disappeared over the hill than we kids began our usual ritual of all the things we weren't allowed to do under parental supervision. We could always get around Mrs. Wigginton, who came to stay with us, and we did just about as we pleased.

First, one of the small brothers was dispatched post-haste to the back field to hunt up a guinea's nest. I had learned to make boiled custard, and we all agreed we'd never had enough—whipped cream and all!

"Take along a long-handled spoon to dig the eggs out with," I said. Funny thing about these shy—and now quite scarce—modestly gray fowl, imported in their wild state from Africa long ago. They make their nests in a deep scratched-out hole in the ground in deep weeds and grass, far away from any buildings, and they would never go back to a nest if the rich, brown, small eggs were removed from the nest by hand. Hence the long-handled spoon.

After we'd had our fill of the rich custard, our next prank was a visit to the attic to open Mother's big Saratoga trunk, which we had been warned never to go into. Out came Mother's brown, beruffled and draped taffeta wedding dress and a parasol with a curved ivory handle, beflounced in yards of black lace and satin. Then out came what we thought to be out of this world for beauty: a moss-covered flower pot with an artificial pink geranium, which we then put on the mantelpiece downstairs.

My sister, Hazel, had a yen for a stuffed bluebird, which she proceeded to adorn her Sunday hat with, and which later proved our undoing, because, while we were parading out under the big old horse apple trees in all our finery, the stuffed bluebird somehow became detached from Hazel's headgear and Mother found it several days later, wet and ruined. That was the end of the treasure chest forays.

Well, I reckon after we'd done about all the mischief we wanted to do and began to feel a little guilty, we began planning to have a big old-timey supper for the folks when they came home. We decided we'd just have to have a big fine watermelon or two from the Frenchman's garden. We didn't have any money, though, and the Frenchman sold his melons in town for a

Sally Lee Phillips outside Hill House, 1944. *Courtesy of Robin Phillips.*

good price. And moreover, we young'uns stood slightly in awe of the black-bearded Frenchman.

We were afraid to ask him for a melon, but then it hit me! We'd go across the creek and get a big feed sack full of the fine yellow pumpkins in the east field and trade them to him for the melons. We tugged them along and "histed" them over the cross fence separating the two farms. Suddenly my two small brothers got cold feet over the project and took off in high gear for home, leaving me to consummate the rest of the business transaction.

Bent on going through with it, I went on and found the Frenchman sitting on a stump above his quaint split-log cabin. He was putting leather half-soles on his shoes with little wooden shoe pegs. He did look pretty fierce, and I forgot all I was going to say. Speechless, I turned the sack upside down and remember yet the way those pumpkins looked rolling off downhill, much to the surprise and consternation of Louis Quesnel. Still I couldn't utter nary a word.

Then, in his broken patois, the Frenchman said, "For why do you bring me the punk?"

"Well," I says, "to eat, maybe." Hopefully now, I'd found my speech!

"Ah. No, Mademoiselle Helene," he said. "I no like-a de punk."

Then I 'lowed, "Feed them to your cattle."

109

"Ah, no," he said. "My cattle no eat-a de punk."

I reckon by then the Frenchman sensed there was more to this talk than would appear. He said, "The small mademoiselle want something, yes?"

Then I told him about the big supper we'd planned and that we didn't have anything for dessert unless we could have one of his melons, because we'd used up all the cream, milk, and eggs for several gallons of boiled custard, which had been consumed. With that, the gallant Frenchman laid aside his shoe mending, went up to his garden, thumped all the melons until he found one ripe, put it over the fence for me and bid me adieu.

And so it was that when the folks came driving in that night, they found the table laid with Great-Grandmother's best linen tablecloth and the best dishes and silverware, and with Ms. Wigginton's roasted hen and all the fixin's. Everything went off fine.

"But where, Helen, did you get the melon?" Dad asked.

"Jes' growed somewhere," I said.

The Frenchman left many years later as quietly as he'd come, still a man of mystery because never did he allude to his family, place of birth, or friends "back yonder" in his homeland. He just came through our backyard one morning on his way to Asheville, he said. His small canvas knapsack tied to the end of his walking stick and slung across his shoulder, he told us goodbye. But as to where he was going, the only answer we got was a smile and a wave of his hand as he went out of sight over the Black Rock trail—a silent and lonely figure of a man, and a gentleman if there ever was one.

THE LOST GOLD MINER

One day back in the '40s, I was busy down at the old place taking up an old linoleum floor covering in the dining room. Took a notion I'd paint the floor a cheerful Chinese red. Mean job taking up old linoleum on account of the tacks and nails to pull out. Just as I was tangling with an old rusty nail with aid of a chisel and a hammer, Dad walked in and said, "You sure take after your mammy's folks. When the Frosts took a notion to do something, there was no peace 'til it was done."

"Well, sir," I 'lowed, "you don't need to feel like you ought to help, Dad. Just pull up a chair and talk to me while I work. 'Twon't take long."

So Dad pulled up his favorite chair and lit his pipe in readiness for a comfortable chat.

"Whatever became of that gold miner who came to Grandfather's house back before the Civil War, Dad?" I said.

"Why, that feller, I've wondered many a time what in the world became of him. His name was Kelly, as I remember. I've still got his fine tools out there in the tool house. He left them when he rode away one morning from your grandfather's house. He rode away on a fine black horse. Had a fine saddle all trimmed in silver, and his horse's bridle was silver-trimmed, too. He sure was an elegant sort of man. A man of property, I'd say. Well-mannered, too. Came from up North somewhere, but at no time or place did he ever give an inkling of exactly where he hailed from, nor was there any mention of kinsmen or friends. After he'd gone away, never to return, we never did find even a scrap of paper among his things to indicate his origin.

"It all comes back to me now," Dad continued. "The man's business down in the Cove was gold mining, and by the way he went at it he must have had a lot of money. He hired a lot of men to mine down in the old fields. They turned the Still-Tub branch that goes down off old Chestnut Mountain on the east into ditches, using big wooden troughs set in riffle boxes, and near 'bout did away with the old fields down the road toward the Georgia line below the Mack Edwards place. He paid off his men every Saturday in solid gold coin, which he carried in his leather saddle bags. Reckon he wasn't too well pleased, though. There was some gold, but not enough to pay. Anyway, seems word got around about the gold rush at the Dahlonega, Georgia, mines, rich beyond all belief."

The John C. Calhoun mine there had just been discovered, and unbelievably rich it was. It's little known, but a certain fact, that the gold from the Calhoun mine was the nucleus of the money that started the South's now-famous Clemson College. Clemson married John C.'s daughter.[*] The college was Clemson's idea, but it was that fiery statesman John C. Calhoun who provided the money for it. Money that was derived from the Dahlonega mine. My late father-in-law, Captain Norris of Anderson, South Carolina, was an intimate friend of Calhoun's, and he often mentioned it. But as usual, I've wandered away from my story.

"Well," Dad continued, "the gold miner left all his wonderful collection of tools with your grandfather. Also left several barrels of sugar, flour, bags of green coffee, and salt. He said he'd be back in a few days, that he'd just ride

---

[*] Thomas Green Clemson (1807–1888), the founder of Clemson Agricultural College (now Clemson University), married Anna Maria Calhoun (1817–1875), whose father, John C. Calhoun (1782–1850), was a congressman and senator from South Carolina, as well as secretary of war, secretary of state and the nation's seventh vice president.

on over to Dahlonega (the name is, by the way, pure Cherokee for "yellow metal") and see for himself what was going on. Well, he just never came back, and that lot of rations came in mighty good during the Civil War when people were parching acorns for coffee and raking the dirt up from their smokehouses to leach out the salt from their meat curing. There was no salt to be had for a long time during the war."

"Well, Dad," I says, "if you've finished your tale, I'll tell mine. Old Easter, when she was helping Mother 'round the house, said one day that Mr. Kelly's horse, saddle, and bridle were sold in Walhalla the day after he'd gone away and that someone waylaid him down there near the Georgia line, below the Old Fields Place mine. She said they did away with him, took his saddle bags full of gold and sold the horse, saddle, and bridle next day. And furthermore, Dad, Easter said that on dark and rainy nights, generally on the 'dark o' the moon,' if a person was passing by that old branch that runs 'longside the old muster and parade grounds where the boys held their maneuvers to join the Confederacy, that right on that branch was where Mr. Kelly was killed and that a light could be seen moving slowly underwater. She also said that sometimes one could hear a bell ringing slowly and mournfully."

Dad sort of laughed then and said, "Easter just liked to tell scary tales." Be that as it may, I near did get scared out of my wits on account of that yarn—years later, that was.

Long back about 1938 it was. I'd suddenly decided to take my baby and come up to the Cove, to the old home to see Mother and Dad. I was with my brother Harry, who was driving a pickup truck. He'd been down to Greenville, where we lived, and we left one stormy October afternoon. As we were coming up from Walhalla after dark, Harry took a notion to take that discarded old road into Horse Cove. It was hardly ever traveled, but it was shorter than coming around through Highlands. It was a deserted, winding road, with not a soul living anywhere on it for miles until it reached the Old Fields gold mine, a mile or two below the Cove.

It was a dark and weirdly lonely night, with dense fog, but the sturdy little old truck trucked along, until it stopped on a bridge of slabs and logs. Harry noticed he'd lost a chain off the back wheel. He got out and started back to look for it, against me making noises as how I didn't want to be left alone with the baby. For suddenly, as I looked upstream, I realized that it was the old muster ground branch where Easter 'lowed Mr. Kelly had been done away with so long ago. Visions of "hants" began to crowd in, and what with the northwest winds howling in the forest and giant chestnut trees bending to

From left: Sally Lee Phillips, Sally Sloan Phillips, Helen Jeanne Turner, Dorothy Norris
Turner and Robin Phillips *(front)* at Hill House. *Courtesy of Robin Phillips.*

the roar of the storm, I wrapped the blanket closer around little Frank and waited in a silence so deep one could almost hear it.

Then it was there. I looked up the branch and I saw *it*: a small light following the meanderings of the rocky little stream. Every now and then there also came a clear ringing sound like a bell! I was now a true believer in ghosts.

There was nothing to do but wait, and in a few minutes my brother jauntily came into sight, swinging the tire chains. They, too, made a bell sound as they clanked together. Shakily, I told him the chains sounded just like the bell I had heard ringing, and that as sure as God made little green apples, the old tale of the dark deed of Mr. Kelly's strange disappearance was true.

"Now, 'bout that light," said my brother. "It sure looks as though it's under the water."

"Did you see it, too?" I says.

"I saw it," 'lowed Henry as he climbed into the truck cab.

"Well what is it?" I said, still shivering.

"Durned if I know," said Harry as he turned on the switch. "Old Easter's ghost, I reckon."

THE MOLASSES GOT AWAY

What with folks busy closing up their summer places—what with some still coming and going, and we the ever present reluctant to say farewell to summer and mountain vacationland—we "inlanders" feel sort of inclined to rest a spell and sort of take stock of things in general while we take it easy like.

Reckon fall, and the spicy apple-laden air—the roadsides still flowering in royal-blue wild asters and saffron-yellow goldenrod (there are seven different varieties of this) and the call of a business-like crow as he flies over a ripened cornfield—we housekeepers, busy in a fragrant, spice-filled kitchen aroma, as pickles, jams, and jellies go into jars and freezing cartons, are thankful and happy over the bounteous yield of field and orchard.

Comes school time and out in the old farmhouse kitchen, busy with tomatoes, corn, and peppers for winter use, I fell someway as usual to "remembering" about the Highlands school days. Back then, there were no bright-orange school buses to pick up the children in outlying coves and valleys, so that some of the children, living too far to come and go daily, oftentimes rented rooms, or their parents did for them, in town. These students would do what we now call lighthouse keeping or, as the kids used to say, "batching it."

I remember Emma Jolly from down on Cullasaja near Franklin and Carrie Edwards, Ann Green, and many others. Carrie and Ann had room in Shortoff in the Jule Phillips home and went to Miss Wells's private school there. Emma Jolly stayed at the Rideouts', where the Catholic church is now.* Come to think of it, I guess Highlands must have had mighty good schools even back then for the young folks to come in from outlying places.

What I started out to tell, though, was the time Mr. Bill Russell, from down toward Walhalla, and whose descendants still own the splendid river bottom farm along both sides of the beautiful Chattooga River at the North Carolina–South Carolina state line, brought his three children—Jim, Ida, and Callie—to live with the Staubs at the cottage (currently at Horse Cove Road and Sixth Street) owned by Mr. and Mrs. Lewis Rice, to go to school. Mrs. Staub, whom many will remember having a generous and loving nature, growing fond of the three youngsters, let them use her big, sunny kitchen with its big, open fireplace and cookstove for preparing their meals. Their father brought their provisions up from the farm every two or three weeks.

---

* The Rideout House, later known as the Satulah House, was a twenty-one-room boardinghouse that stood roughly on the site of the Our Lady of the Mountains Catholic church on North Fifth Street.

Ida, busy one real cold Saturday morning baking for the week ahead, up and tells Jim to take a big milk pan out to the smokehouse and draw a gallon or two of molasses from the hundred-gallon barrel stored out there. She was baking gingerbread. Reckon it being cold and all, the sweet stuff ran out kind of slow-like, and Jim, young'un-like, leaves the pan setting under the bunghole to fill and takes off outside to whittle on his slingshot.

Ida became impatient over the delay since he'd been gone a right smart while, and she proceeded to cross the yard and open the smokehouse door and was pushed back by a wall of thick black molasses! Majestically, with silent dignity, like a flow of lava from Mount Vesuvius it rolled, and riding along the crest of the mass quite serenely were five of Mrs. Staub's fall-hatched fluffy baby chicks, accompanied by a squawking, frustrated dominecker hen.

'Bout that time, of all things, up drove the kids' pa with their weekly supply of rations. He drove right square up to the kitchen door, the mules trying to sidestep the lake of molasses and sort of actin' up. Mrs. Staub, telling me about it when I was a little girl years later, laughing over it still, said Mr. Russell was just about the maddest man she'd ever laid eyes on, 'cept of course the time when the Yankees rode off down in Georgia with her father's best saddle horse during the Civil War.

A cottage off Walking Stick Road in Horse Cove, circa 1890s. *Courtesy of Robin Phillips.*

He 'lowed he'd teach 'em to lay waste to one hundred gallons of the best molasses he'd ever made and he reached for his leather-thonged bullwhip, but the young'uns had disappeared into back of beyond.

Mrs. Staub said they had to send for Dolph Picklesimer and his team and wagon, and it took nearly a day to haul in enough dirt to cover that mess o' molasses.

SATULAH MOUNTAIN TREMBLED

One wonders sometimes about lots of things in the mountains. They seem to hold a sort of mystery.

There's the time old Mr. Dolph Picklesimer from over Clear Creek way came to Grandfather's house one winter's day long 'bout this time of the year. He said he was hog hunting. You see, in those days of free range for stock, a feller's hogs grew fat and sassy on the now long-extinct chestnut mast, and all he had to do when meat got scarce was to take his hog rifle and a couple of dogs, kill what hogs he needed, and "sled" 'em home from the abundant forests. Chestnut-fattened pork back then was near 'bout the best eating on earth. Such backbones, spareribs, and sausage!

Anyway, after Dolph had passed the time of day with my Grandfather, he 'lowed as how "Old Stooly"—Satulah Mountain—"just near 'bout got me scared to death here lately, Squire Hill. That fool mountain's acting awful strange, seems like. I swear to goodness, I was right up under it above my house a day or two back and kept hearing a sort of rumbling racket.

"It 'peared like it was coming from the inside of the mountain," he said in an awesome whisper.

Instead of taking this statement lightly from a man my grandfather knew to be absolutely sober and truthful, he remembered that when he was helping to remove the Cherokees from the mountain wilderness when he was commissioned by General Winfield Scott,* an old chief spoke of Satulah rather grimly. "No go there," he'd say. "Mountain, he make bad noise. He rumbling mountain."

"I was up there getting firewood," Dolph went on, "right under the mountain, and kept hearing a rumbling, groaning sound. And there wasn't a

---

* Winfield Scott (1786–1866) was an army general who, in 1838, supervised the removal of the Cherokees from North Carolina and other southern states to reservations west of the Mississippi River.

Black Rock Mountain in Horse Cove. *Courtesy of Helen Hill Norris family.*

whisper o' wind. I put my ear down to a rock in a cliff, and that noise, sure as God made little green apples, was coming from the inside of the mountain. Seemed like I smelt sulfur, too.

"I went on up toward the cliff we've always called 'toadstool,' and blessed if the rocks weren't hot. Hot enough that I could feel it plumb through my shoe soles. It was a cold day, too. Then it seemed that the ground would sort of shake now and then just a little."

Grandpa was curious by this time, I reckon, for he saddled up his horse and went on home with Dolph, and except for a faint, far-off roaring, which seemed to be coming from a few cracks in the mountain, it seemed to hold no menace, and for centuries on end the old mountain from its lofty height still guards the southern approach to the now-famous Highlands plateau.

The "old folks" say that, way back in the 1880s, during the time of the Charleston earthquake,* Satulah, along with Old Whiteside and Black Rock, acted up something fearful. It was in August, as well as I can recall. Dad said 1885, and the old hotel, now long since gone, was full of

---

* On August 31, 1885, a powerful earthquake struck near Charleston, South Carolina, causing extensive damage to the city and sixty deaths.

summer guests, mostly General Wade Hampton's family and others from Charleston and Columbia, South Carolina. When the second quake-shock came—very severe, just a few minutes—the mysterious sounds coming from Black Rock near 'bout scared some of the folks out of their wits. Some of the gals fainted. Dishes, pots, and pans rattled. Pictures fell from the walls. It sort of panicked everybody for a little while, and by the time we children came along, folks were wont to reckon local happenings "from the time of the earthquake."

ONE MORNING IN JUNE

It was just "out of this world," that far-off morning in June. I was home for the summer from Greenville with my four children, and Dad took a notion to saddle up the two little tough mules and take me way over beyond the Chattooga River country. We left the kids with Mother.

Dad had sort of gotten interested in some columns I was doing at the time for the *Greenville News*, and running out of answers to my questions, I reckon, he remembered Granny McCall, whose father came to Horse Cove long before my ancestors, and "Granny" was one who remembered.

I hadn't been able to get beyond the 1830s to save me, and I wanted to know more about what this wildly beautiful country was like before Grandfather came, when he was commissioned by General Winfield Scott, along with Colonel J.H. Alley of Whiteside Cove, to move the gentle, picturesque Cherokees over to the Indian reservation. I always hated that. Guess Grandmother did, too, because a little Indian girl got away with a papoose* on her back, took out over the end of Black Rock Mountain, and hid in the woods for three weeks. Grandmother fed her and the baby and took blankets to her. Finally, one of the braves came back for her. It was a blot on our family escutcheon, nothing else—those harmless children of nature living peacefully in our little closed-in valley.

Down we went, through rhododendron in full and lavish bloom, on the trail to Ellicott's Rock in the middle of the Chattooga River, where the states of North Carolina, South Carolina, and Georgia "cornered," marked in the early part of the century by a government surveyor named Ellicott. We let our mules rest and browse while we ate our lunch, and blessed if that crystal river wasn't plumb full of fish! They'd rise to most anything we'd throw

---

* A term, now used mostly in historical contexts, for a Native American baby.

Mary Ann Oatman Stevens Frost, wife of Dr. Charles Leonard Frost and mother of Sarah Apalonia Frost. *Courtesy of Robin Phillips.*

in the water, and it near 'bout laid Dad out because he hadn't brought his fishin' pole along, even though it was Sunday.

The trail got steep and narrow going out on the eastern rim, and it was sort of scary, with the river below roaring and dashing over and around huge boulders on its mad rush to the sea. It was awesomely beautiful, though, and when we looked at the sunlit fields, with the cows grazing and the smoke curling from Granny's big log cabin chimney, it was somehow comforting and peaceful.

She sat near the front door, wearing a long white apron with a wide hem in the bottom and three tucks above it that covered her neat print dress.

That was the pioneer settlement of Bull Pen, and once a lot of folks lived there. It's a "Goldsmith's Deserted Village" now and has long since fallen into the limbo of the past. The picturesque hewn log cabins have tumbled down, and the fields have been reclaimed by the forest.

She was tickled to death to see Dad, whom she'd played with when she was a little girl when Dave Morgan, her father, lived in what was later Grandfather's place and is now the Colonel Howe estate in the Cove. She sent a grandchild to bring us fresh water from the spring. (Beats all how the mountain-born always show a spark of hospitality—albeit nothing but a drink of fresh water.)

Dad and Granny passed the time of day, that being inquiries as to the health and well-being of each and every member of the family, and how the crops were doing, etc., for one would by no manner or means come right out with the object of their visit until these amenities were over with. That would be a bad breach of manners and show a lack o' "proper raisin'." Finally, Dad got her started, very cleverly I thought, as he tilted his chair back on two legs against the wall, lit his pipe, and pulled his hat down to shade his eyes.

"Don't much like to talk about things way back yonder," Granny 'lowed as she shooed a chicken rooster off the doorstep. "Aim to put that rooster in a pot one o' these days. Seems like every time anybody comes, he hops up here on the doorstep and starts crowing. Like every other male thing 'round here, reckon he has to have the floor.

"Mainly," she went on, "nobody listens to old folks talk anymore. Dave Morgan, my pa, came up here long 'bout 1820, best I can 'reckelect.' Wasn't a sign of a road, either. He sort of hacked out trees and bushes as we went along. Drove our old ox hitched to a two-wheeled cart, with Ma holding the baby in her lap an' doin' the drivin', while Pa himself drove our milk cow and a couple o' sheep, and Joe, my brother, and I drove the hogs.

"We didn't have much to do with," she continued, "just a cross-cut saw, a double-bitted axe, a hammer, and a couple of iron wedges, or go-devils, to split logs with. That was about all. We made out, though, and built right across there at the foot of Rich's mountain by a good spring. Didn't have any nails, o' course, but Pa and the boys raised the walls in no time, notched them to fit at the corners, and drove big wooden pegs through 'em. Then they rived out big, wide, 36-inch-long shakes from logs and covered that cabin by laying them on poplar pole rafters, weighing them down with poles laid longways and tied down at the corners with split hickory bark. I think they laid big flat rocks from the creek on top of the poles, too. Pa 'adzed' off with the axe one side of some big logs for a puncheon floor. Then they built a good fireplace where we did the cookin'.

"There wasn't a nail in that house nowhere," she continued, "and it was as good and stout and warm a house as you'd ever see anywhere. No windows, though. Glass windows was plumb never heard of, 'cept maybe someplace far off. We had wooden shutters to openings in the walls, with hinges made out of cowhide leather. Good, stout shutters.

"You see, honey," she went on, "this country was plumb full o' 'painters' [panthers], wildcats, and wolves then. The night my little brother was born, I remember Pa fastening the shutters down tight. Ma was wanting them open for air, and Pa saying 'Nay.' The cow was carryin' on out at the milking gap, and the other stock was restless. There was a 'painter' or sumthin' around for sure.

"We made our first crop with a plow cut out of the heart of a locust stump—a good one, too. Pa made the plow handles, and we all took turns pullin' the plow 'cause our old ox took sick, an' he liked as ever was to have died."

Later, going on back home down the "winding stairs," as they are still called, down to the river, through the flower-scented dusk, listening to the sweet liquid notes of my beloved hermit thrush, how grateful I felt for a day like this, which will be always and forever enshrined in my heart.

THE GORGE ROAD

It's an old forgotten and abandoned thing now, that road is, but many's the time it lingers among our childhood memories as a fearsome thing, for it was threaded upward among towering cliffs—trapped forests on one side marching sedately to the crest of Flat Rock Mountain, and a rollicking stream way down below on the other side.

One stirringly colored Indian summer day in October, the month that lures so many back to the hightops, we took off, my sister, Hazel, and I. We wrapped up a sausage biscuit or two and an apple and took off to find the long-lost Gorge Road. On the way, I remembered hearing of an Indian bead mine from some of the help on the farm when we were children. Maybe it was old Mrs. Wigginton, who used to help mother around the house sometimes, who said that one could find beautiful pieces of their work among the deep pits where the old Cherokee arrow-makers chipped away at their spear-and-bird-point arrowheads and made beads to adorn some Indian girl.

I always felt somehow that there was apt to be more truth than fiction in the tale, so as we separated, Hazel going one way and me the other, climbing around over fallen and cut timber and boulders and such, I was thinking about the Indian mine. Then I heard Hazel calling me from a ridge on the left. She had without a doubt found the old mine. There it lay, deep pits dug in the outcropping of the finest specimens I'd ever seen of crystal quartz and feldspar.

Of course, over a hundred years the mine had lain there undisturbed. The tall trees had grown up inside the excavations, and the ever-watchful forest had as usual covered in deep debris the Indians' secret place.

I was so busy digging and throwing off gloves along with caution as I gleefully dug up gorgeous crystalized quartz that I didn't hear my sister yelling, "Helen, for heaven's sake, jump up quick! Don't you see that copperhead right in front of you?"

She vows yet that I never missed a lick with my pick and that I glanced up once and 'lowed, "Yes, it's a copperhead," and went right on digging. Seems I do remember, though, seeing that surprised copperhead disappearing under a rock. In easy reach of me, he had kind of turned, and I'm sure gave me a well-deserved look of disgust as he went out of sight.

Lugging as many specimens as we could carry, we went back down our freshly broken trail to the old road and fell to talking about how the covered wagons coming in from the South Carolina markets always dreaded that bit of road. It lay mostly under ice all winter long, and on the upended road, rock-shelved on the upper side, it sloped sharply on the lower side into a deep and dark ravine. So when it was ice-covered, sometimes the top-heavy covered wagons and horses slid off, carrying the barrels of flour, kerosene, etc., into a tangled mass, and it took a mighty sober "waggoner" to untangle that, which wasn't always the case—being sober, I mean. Reckon if it hadn't been for a "certain place" back down on the river road where a feller could stop for a "nip" or two, the old-timers couldn't have made it at all.

Then we talked on, about how old Mrs. Hawkins thought nothing at all of walking the eight miles from Highlands after dark to her home down beyond, and who had been by the Hill House one night and remained for

Hazel Hill Sloan, age sixteen.
Courtesy of Robin Phillips.

one of those long fireside talks with the folks after supper. How she told about, when going through the gorge, hearing what she thought was her daughter, Laura, coming to meet her and how she'd answered the call. Soon, realizing that the call had become a savage scream and was behind her, she lit out for home, and her menfolks, taking lanterns, lost no time going out in the night to look for a panther. Strange things, panthers; they've very rarely been known to attack a person, but they have a weird way of following humans for miles, plumb curious, I reckon. Our menfolks used to say if a panther found a feller hurt or crippled it would be another story.

Then there's the time when Mother had told us in a hushed sort of voice that we were in real trouble, that Dad had been compelled to borrow—listen to this—the vast sum of fifty dollars. It seemed a fearful thing, for we'd never known or heard of anyone having to borrow that much money.

We straightway began figuring out a way to help Dad out of this very serious matter. We began gathering galax leaves and the ever-graceful evergreen leucothoe sprays. Mother had sent to New York for a copy of *Florists' Review,* and after writing the Kervan Company, which advertised in the magazine, orders began to pile in. We were delighted! I remember Mr. Kervan himself coming down to Hill House. He spent several days with us and showed us how to gather the leaves and pack them.

Then one day, a rush order came from Mr. Kervan for two thousand very small, very perfect, little green galax leaves. Time being the essence of this contract, little Hazel was dispatched one late winter day, bundled up and mittened, to go over to the gorge road where the best small ones grew and bring them in. How we laughed while talking it all over that October day as we trudged homeward with our rocks. She talked about how afraid she was, with the moaning of the wind among the cliff-bound big chestnut trees as they leaned, wind-whipped, against one another, making an eerie, almost human sound. Ah, those dearly loved old chestnut trees, gone now, ghosts of the past.

She also recalled how afraid she was that she might meet the bear Dad had passed on the road one night or the panther Mrs. Hawkins had heard. But the little nine-year-old came trudging solidly home with the two thousand little galax leaves, and it wasn't until long afterward that we were to learn from Kervan that her little galax leaves had been ordered for, and used for, no less an occasion than Alice Roosevelt's famous and beautiful wedding at the White House when she married Nicholas Longworth.[*] They'd been used with purple violets and little nosegays for the placecards at her wedding breakfast.

THE TOOTH DENTIST COMES TO TOWN

This little homespun column's been sort o' laid up lately, what with flu and relapse of same and one thing and another. Sort of marooned out here, too, since the old bridge across the lake is being replaced with our proud new two-way bridge, preparatory to the widening and hard-surfacing of Billy Cabin Road. So for a spell it's just been the chipmunks and the TV and me, out here on the colorful slopes above Mirror Lake.

By the way, those sagacious little chipmunks—smart? You should see them gathering hickory nuts. Saw one or two hefting first one nut and then another in his furry front paws, finally discarding both and scampering about among the leaves for better ones.

---

[*] Alice Roosevelt, a daughter of President Theodore Roosevelt, married Representative Nicholas Longworth of Ohio at the White House on February 17, 1906.

Fell to thinking and remembering back the other day about how severe our colds were when we were children, and of all the fool things poor Mother, not used to pioneering, would do for us under the direction of our dear old resourceful Mrs. Wiggington, who came in by the day and whom we all adored.

There'd be teas brewed and onions roasted. The juice from the onions was mixed with sulfur and ground-ivy tea and squawvine tea (an Indian remedy). Then there'd be flannel chest plasters, soaked in mutton, suet, turpentine, and camphor, these being fastened to our heavy underwear. We'd be admonished not to take 'em off under any circumstances until we were well.

Helen Martense Hill Norris.
Courtesy of Helen Hill Norris family.

Even then, Mrs. Wiggington warned not to take 'em off during the day. They were, she said, to be unfastened when you went to bed and "lost" during sleep! Poor Mother—and poor us—for the misery we endured from the awful itching set up by the plasters. Maybe the consequent scratching and rubbing did some good. Anyway, in spite of it, we'd get well.

Came a time once, though, when no amount of Mrs. Wiggington's remedies did any good, and Dad saddled up the horse and took off for a doctor. He came early the next day—it was on a Sunday, seems like—and Mother put flowers in our rooms and freshened the bed linens, even getting out a very honored and sacred silk quilt of "log cabin" pattern, which was pieced and put together by an aunt back in Locust Valley, Long Island.

When Dr. Anderson got there, Dad stabled and fed his horse, and such a time as they all had, visiting and exchanging news. Mother was busy roasting a wild turkey Dad had shot the day before and setting out the best linen and silver. Don't believe we sick kids upstairs got a bit of attention 'til after dinner.

Doc stayed two or three days—think of it! First thing he did was throw out the teas, then off came the chest plasters. Then there he sat, measuring on the tip of his fine pen knife little doses of Dover's powders and quinine, and wrapping each dose in a paper. How we loved him, and what a big kick Dad and Mother had out of his visit.

Medicos really took it easy then, for there was Doctor Higgins, the dentist, who came twice a year, spring and fall. He set up his dental chair and other instruments of torture right on the hotel porch in town, so that word would get out to the local populace that the dentist was in town. There he'd grind away or pull teeth, the patient (or victim) being stared at by the spectators gathered on the sidewalk in front.

Splendid advertising as word got around the "tooth dentist" was in town!

BEARS

A recent bill introduced at the legislative hall in Raleigh has real teeth in it. Representatives Marcellus Buchanan of Jackson County and Oral L. Yates of Haywood introduced a bill prohibiting the practice of business concerns, principally service stations and gift shops, caging bears and other wild animals along the highways to attract passing tourists and thereby gaining some business.

Seems a joint resolution was made authorizing appointment of a legislative study committee to look into the cruel practice, this being the outcome of the efforts of the two legislators mentioned. It is hoped that something will be done about it soon as possible, for no one who has seen a caged bear pacing back and forth in a narrow, not-too-clean cage, looking longingly toward his natural mountain fastness home, can feel anything but pity for him.

Sort of reminds me, though, of a time when my sympathy for a hungry bear near 'bout got the best of me back in the '30s when, with the young Norrises and some of the Hills, I was touring the West, completely taken up with the wonders of Yellowstone National Park, which I believe was the nation's first.

Along the highway, I spotted a bear, back off the road aways. Leaving the car, under protest from others, I went out quite a little ways to get a closer view of the bruin and to beg an overture toward becoming better acquainted. He started coming right toward me—fast! Guess he thought I might have a candy bar or something, and he struck a dead lope. Having nothing to offer him to eat, I, too, struck out in a dead lope and headed for the road and car, the bear steadily gaining on me meanwhile.

The folks in the car yelled to me to run faster if possible. I began really making tracks until I got within "hollering" distance and told them to throw all the bacon and bread we had in our camp-out box to the bear. As he proceeded to make his meal out of what was to have been our supper, I looked up to find that many tourists had stopped, and to my utter amazement and chagrin they were just dying laughing and making pictures of my race.

But I was glad to beat it into the parked car, much wiser but with some loss of dignity, plus the loss of two pounds of excellent breakfast bacon and several loaves of bread.

Then there was the time a hunter went into the woods without a gun and in an isolated spot came up with a bear! Having no "shootin' irons," he decided to argue it out with the bear, having the idea, as many naturalists have maintained, that a bear has real "super-duper" intelligence. The bear, however, seemed to have other ideas and began growling and showing his immense white teeth. So the man opened the conversation by saying, "Now, now, old man, let's talk this thing over, man to bear."

"But," says the bear, "I'm hungry!"

To which the man says, "Oh, that's nothing. Look at me. I'm out looking for a fur coat for my wife, and I haven't had a chance of getting it. You see, a feller can't always get what he wants,"

So the man and the bear argued back and forth for a while, but it ended up with the bear not being hungry anymore—and the man having the fur coat!

They Dug a Well, or Tried To

Every summer, when my young grown-ups come back home like the swallows returning to Capistrano, I take off in high gear down to the old place in Horse Cove, for the children, having spent all their childhood summers there with their grandparents, won't stay up in Highlands with me. Guess it's OK, 'cept there's so awful much to do, and help is hard to get, everybody busy during the summer months.

So while the wild oats and tough old broomsedge grow rank and tall over the farm acres of lawn and garden, and the air is filled with birdsong, instead of my thoughts "taking the wings of the morning and flying to the uttermost parts of the earth" like the Bible says, my thoughts turn amusedly to the time that Dad and Mother decided to build the house we now live in part of the time and where we all grew up.

"Sallie," Dad says, "there's no water, no spring, no water available at all. It just won't do."

Dad had a love of fresh bubbling spring water, as the mountain-born always do. It was on a Sunday afternoon, I remember, and we'd walked down from the old pioneer six-room log cabin, built by Horse Cove's first settler, Billy Barnes, back before the Civil War, according to our land records. We were virtually camping there until Dad got the house built.

But to get back to my story, Dad and Mother were arguing about the water situation. I can see Mother later at the stove, cooking supper in deep thought. Finally, she comes out the back door, kicking the kitten out of her way, and says to Dad, "Nothing to this water business. We'll simply dig a well."

Poor Dad looked at her, then looked up toward the mountain standing in silent majesty a thousand feet above the level farmland, giving birth from its many-millions-old heart to many cold bubbling springs. Finally Dad said, "Well, we can try it." And so they dug…and dug…on and on…just mud… no water…awful-smelling mud.

Mother, though, nothing daunted her. Finally, she came out with, "It's very simple, Frank. I'm writing my cousin Cliff Woodmelt back in New York to come down here and take this thing over. He knows everything there is to know about wells. We used to have wells on Long Island where Cliff and I grew up."

Guess Mother hadn't heard of such a thing as "water witching" with a forked stick, or she would have latched on to the idea.

Anyway, be that as it may, came Cousin Cliff, who promptly decided to stop operations on the site by the proposed back door and move fifty feet back. Well, time and dirt flew, and still no water, just great buckets of mud and slime coming up on the winding windlass.

Finally, the men took to the woods, cut down several big, strong hollow trees, and proceeded to sink them down into a sixty-foot hole in the ground. Reckon the idea was to keep the mud out. Anyway, Cousin Cliff, all excited, goes down on a rope, trying to place the caissons. He had on hip-length boots, too, and just "terreckly," as Uncle Remus would say of Br'er Rabbit, we heard yelling from down in the well. Things evidently weren't doing so well with Cousin Cliff.

Mother called Sam, our hired man, and he went down on another rope, and blessed if he wasn't just in time to jerk Cousin Cliff loose from a sudden death in quicksand. The log caissons had already gone under, plumb out of sight. Cousin Cliff was yanked to the surface, minus his rubber boots, minus his trousers, and minus most everything 'cept what the English would call "his small clothes."

Cousin Cliff took off in a day or so, back to New York and a more sophisticated life, but Dad, with Mother's cheerful encouragement, not long afterward got a pump, and we finally had water coming in from a neighboring spring.

However, it's interesting to note, in later years I learned by writing to various and sundry departments in Washington that my beloved Horse Cove was, millions and millions of years ago, a very, very deep, deep valley, pointed at the bottom, sort of. A lecturer at our Biological Research Station here told me that when our six mountains that stand guard through the centuries over the little "hanging valley" were first pushed up through Earth's crust, approximately twenty feet of earth crested their lofty top, which, again through the centuries, washed down and filled the deep sunken valley with alluvial earth, so that there could not possibly be underground streams such as are found in other high plateaus.

THEY JUST ABOUT DROWNED

These days are unprecedented hot ones. It's a shame to have to go "off the mountain" on errands, "horrorsome," going south to Walhalla, which I had to do to get a new refrigerator when mine just treacherously tuckered out during this hot spell.

Noticed little numbered stakes along the road and found in going that the "powers that be" are fixing to widen this much-used highway by four feet to the Chattooga River Bridge, which is practically the South Carolina state line. Also, the very smooth paving will be used in the resurfacing of this, such as the South Carolinians used from their state line to Walhalla. It'll be fine.

Getting on to the inner bridge down the road, we remembered Mother telling us 'bout the time she first came south from New York in the late '70s, a young girl just graduated from our great-uncle's Quaker College at Locust Valley, Long Island, New York. She was a classmate of Sir Winston Churchill's mother, Jennie Jerome, who married Lord Randolph Churchill.

I remember, too, the intimate little stories mother told us of Jennie's—Lady Churchill's—visit back home, bringing Sir Winston, a belligerent little boy who she said "fit and fought" every small boy on the street. A born fighter, bless him! What a statesman! Absolutely without parallel. Do so hope he's making it, lying over there in bed with that broken leg.[*]

But of "time and river" now. There was no bridge at all over the river then. Mother and her father, the late Dr. Charles Frost of New York, had spent the night at the "Halfway House," the Russell Farm. One couldn't

---

[*] Former Prime Minister Winston Churchill of Britain fell in his room in a hotel in Monte Carlo on June 28, 1962, fracturing the neck of his left femur.

Dr. Charles Leonard Frost (1821–1893). After he graduated from the Columbia University School of Physicians and Surgeons, he and a brother sailed around Cape Horn to California during the gold rush and opened a general store in Auburn, California, to supply materials to the miners. Charles married Mary Ann Oatman Stevens, and they had two children, Sarah and Charles Jr. After his wife's death, Charles returned to Long Island, where his mother raised the children while he practiced medicine. When he began to have health problems around 1889, he moved to Highlands with his grown daughter, Sarah Apalonia Frost. He continued to practice medicine until his death. *Courtesy of Helen Hill Norris family.*

make it from the Southern Railway in Seneca, South Carolina, to Highlands in one day, you see. It took about a day and a half.

It had been raining a long time. There was that turbulent, rushing Chattooga plumb out of its banks and all over the big, flat river-bottom corn lands every which way you looked. Couldn't even see where the road was. Swift, swishing currents of water. The driver of the three-seated hack, a "carryall" in New England, didn't want to try the crossing, but Grandfather Frost, anxious to get to his new home in Highlands, urged the poor old scared driver on. Mother was holding on tight to the seat. Here came the water flooding into the hack. Horses began swimming and washing downstream, losing their footing completely.

Mother, scared plumb to death, gathered up her skirts and, leaving the outfit, jumped into waist-deep water and ran way down the big field where Mr. Russell was ploughing on a sloping hillside. Mr. Russell, poor man, liked never to have made out what on earth was the matter, but when he did— from mother's excited hand-waving, mostly, I reckon—he went into action. Taking no time to unhitch his big mules, with a few whacks of his knife he cut them loose, and leading one and riding the other, got to the flooded team, the hack, and the two badly scared men. Again taking his knife, he cut the two swimming and struggling horses loose from their hampering harness so they could swim out. Then he carried the two men out on his two mules, leaving the hack alone 'til the river ran down to normal.

The Highlands mail was often delayed back then during the heavy rains. Mail time being the event of the day, everybody would gather at the post office around 4:30 in the afternoon. It wasn't at all unusual for a rider on horseback, coming in from lower down, to tell us the river was out of banks and there'd be no mail until the next day.

Speaking of the matter of mail, last year while I was in New York waiting for the *Queen Elizabeth* to leave for my trip to England and the continent with my two daughters, I was so intrigued by the inscription across the classic Greek portal over the U.S. Post Office that I memorized it: "Neither snow nor rain nor heat nor gloom of night stays these couriers from the swift completion of their appointed rounds."

I bethought me of our own Gene Mayes and his forty years over bad and unpaved roads, as well as other faithful carriers of Uncle Sam's mail in the mountains.

Anyway, home. "God gave all men the earth to love, but since our hearts are small, ordained for each one spot should prove beloved over all." That's Rudyard Kipling's, not mine.

OLD CHRISTMAS

I joined an in-gathering of the Hill clan at my cousin Mary Hill Bearden's home in upper South Carolina, and somehow the talk got around to Christmas.

Mary, whose excellent memory of bygone days and times is intriguing, was telling us 'bout one Christmas when she was a little girl. Seems back then, near 'bout everybody in wintertime galloped around on horseback on account of bad roads. One snowbound day, her dad and mine, who were brothers, took off to way over toward Clayton, Georgia, spending Christmas at the Scruggs'. Mary said she reckoned they'd wore out their welcome and eaten up all the Christmas "fixin's" 'bout the third day. They came on down to Grandfather Hill's in Horse Cove and started having "second Christmas."

Guess Grandpa got sort of fed up, what with the big dance frolic every night, and Grandma and old Dan, a former slave from Eastern Carolina, worn out with so much cooking. The party had increased to about fifteen boys and girls. Well, when Grandpa told 'em off, it sure didn't break up the party. No sir! They sort of held a council, then away they went, a merry, laughing group, all on horseback, over the hill and away to Whiteside Cove to Colonel J.H. Alley's home (the late Judge Felix Alley's home). They awakened the Colonel, got him out of bed even, and told him they'd come for the last "Twelve Days of Christmas."

It was a tradition for many years here in the mountains that "Old Christmas" was kept, lasting until January 6 of the new year. I sort of think it was the custom in other places in the Carolinas, too, because I remember my beloved mother-in-law, Mrs. J.K. Norris of Anderson, South Carolina, spoke of their plantation holding and keeping the "Twelve Days of Christmas," now immortalized in song and story.

Well, getting back to my story, the Colonel 'lowed, "Well, boys, you've come to the wrong place this time. We've all been sick, and nobody's been able to go to the mill to have meal ground. We've not even been well enough to kill our hogs, and there's not a stick of wood cut."

"What of it" quoth the merry, undaunted young folks. "Go on back to bed, Colonel. We'll take over."

So it was that axes and saws started buzzing, and the woodpile was built up in a short time, while other young fellers were out at the corncrib shelling golden ears of corn for the trip to the mill. Further along in the bright, sunlit morning, four fat hogs were hanging, ready to be cut up into backbones and spareribs and sausage. The Christmas party, now on its third round, was on the go again.

Those were the days. In the land of bright waters, land of the mountains, the cliff, and the dell; health to their sons, long life to their daughters, and peace to the homes where the mountaineers dwell.

UNCLE CHARLEY'S DOG AND EAGLE

Highlands birdwatchers are having a ball this winter. Cold like it is, and the little feathered friends flocking in from the forests and fields to our feeders, sort of keeps a feller busy putting out feed and scattering small grain.

It's fun to watch them. Like people, they seem to have different personalities. Now take that pair of red birds. The gallant little red-coated feller sits patiently out on the edge of the woodland, while his more somber-hued mate enjoys her breakfast at the feeder. Not until the lady has finished and carefully cleaned her pink bill and had her morning dip in the birdbath does the southern gentleman deign to fly in for his breakfast. But sometimes if his ladybird has trouble cracking her sunflower seed, he'll fly down and crack it for her and feed her. Well, the ways of birds and "of mice and men" are a never-ending wonder anyway.

Fodderstack Mountains as seen from Uncle Buck's home. *Courtesy of Robin Phillips.*

Some years ago, when I was living down in the Cove at the summer home my husband, the late John J. Norris, and I built, I came around to the back of the house quietly to take some things off the clothesline and was amazed to see a tremendous bald eagle sitting out on a dead chestnut limb overhanging our small clear lake.

I'd been reading and sort of "honing up" on eagles and ravens, so first thought I'd slip in the back door for my camera. Then, for fear I'd make a noise or a move that would break up the almost unbelievable scene, I eased down to the doorstep, screened by the hedge, and waited to see just what would happen. Then, very soon, those great, gray wings spread swiftly, silently, and *bam!* The little lake was minus a beautiful big speckled trout, which came up thrashing wildly in the eagle's talons.

Instead of taking off into the wild forested slopes of Fodderstack Mountain, blessed if that great emblem of liberty of our nation didn't fly low to the rock-walled barbecue pit, and there he proceeded to whip his catch against the rocks until he laid him out. Then it was I went and got my book *The American Bald Eagle* and learned that the bald eagle is the only predatory bird that kills his prey before he eats it.

I remember a tale Dad used to tell about young Uncle Charley Hill, who often, to quote, "went up the airy mountain and down the rushy glen. A man who would a-hunting go." Up the trail over Sagee, where our flock of sheep used to come in single file down the mountainside for their weekly salt in the barnyard, and up and across the Bowery, following the old bear trail to the top of Black Rock, Uncle Charley went on that fair summer day, his small yellow cur squirrel dog leading along in front. Gip, his name was, and the menfolks thought a lot of him for he knew exactly how to "turn" a squirrel. That means just barking a little at Mr. Squirrel and giving him the notion to run down the far side of the tree where the man waited with his gun.

Gip, going ahead of Uncle Charley, came out on a high moss-covered cliff overlooking the valley below. There was a clear blue sky overhead, and the man and dog stopped to rest and enjoy the view. Suddenly, from overhead, a swift and silent shadow fell across them. There was a gentle whirring of ruffled wings. Looking up alarmed, Uncle Charley saw the outstretched wings of a bald eagle, with his head and wicked eyes fastened on the little dog.

Realizing that he was about to lose Gip to the eagle, he fired his gun and maimed the eagle enough so that he fell to the edge of the cliff. Gip pounced on him in no time at all, and then began the battle royal. Round and round they went, the tough little cur holding on and not giving an inch. But soon the eagle, with his huge wingbeat and cruel claws, forced Gip to the brink of the rock that hung out over the valley below, a thousand feet down.

Seems Uncle Charley eased himself around sort of under the edge of the cliff and, finding a toehold to cling to, reached up and waited for his chance to grab the little dog, still fighting mad, by the hind leg. He tied him fast to his hunting belt, then fired and finished off the huge bird.

It was all he could do, Dad said, to drag the eagle home and carry Gip. The little cur was all scratched up and hurt real bad. Later, when the bald eagle was stretched out on the lawn at home, General Wade Hampton, the wartime governor of South Carolina, who visited Grandfather Hill during the summer season, got his rule, and measured the emblem of American liberty. Dad said from wingtip to wingtip it measured twenty-five feet. However, Dad said with a twinkle in his eye, "We Hills are always inclined to stretch things a little to make a good story."

Eager Beavers

Comes now a farewell to summer. Seldom has our lofty highland country had such a beautiful season: glory of blue skies overhead, while road and trail and pathways have been full of travelers.

According to a recent communication, our Highlands will be visited this week by U.S. Supreme Court Justice William O. Douglas, who has been climbing mountains since his boyhood. He will be accompanied by James K. Vessey, southern regional forester, and Harvey Broome of Knoxville, Tennessee, president of the American Wilderness Society.

On his way to Highlands, Justice Douglas plans to take in the fourteen-thousand-acre wildlife area now proposed by the U.S. Forest Service.[*] This area lies in Transylvania County and would be the second such wildlife area in the South, the other being in the Linville Gorge Section.[†]

Speaking of wildlife and its protection, come the protection of those busy, eager little old beavers down here in the Cove. Blest if they haven't just near about taken over in some places down here on the creek that flows southward through the valley, tumbling at last over the waterfall at the lower end of the Cove on its way to the sea.

I kept hearing from the kids about how the beavers had built dams along the creek, so I took off down Walking Stick Road the other day with my folks. We turned off right on a level stretch of road before coming to the falls, and through a tangle of blackberry, pokeberry, and wild grapevines, we made our way to an abandoned creek bed, to where long ago Mrs. Webb had her milking gap where the cows came down from the pasture to be milked each evening, close to where the Morgans, who had settled in the Cove around 1820, built the very first human habitation.

We had to take off our shoes there and wade across the rippling, laughing, pebbled stream. We sat down on the other side to dry our feet and put our shoes on again and then started on the cutest little fairy-like trail, barely visible, to find one skillfully engineered dam after another.

Never underestimate the little beaver's ability! They had actually cut down small saplings, felling them across the stream at a logically selected spot, generally on a curve of the stream. They don't cut their trees straight across clean. It's a pointed stump, woven in and out with infinite care, with loads of branches and twigs that are anchored down in the bed of the creek with firmly packed mud.

---

* Believed to now be part of the Pisgah National Forest.

† The Linville Gorge Wilderness area, part of the Pisgah National Forest.

I counted eight such dams as we fought our way on up toward the open meadows through tangles of underbrush. And here began the flooding of the meadows. This being on the Howe property, and the meadows and the swamps highly prized by visiting biologists at the research station in Highlands, it is the last stronghold of much plant life that through the ages has disappeared through drainage of fields and meadows and by cultivation.

Mrs. James Howe became somewhat concerned over the flooded meadowland. I found to her delight, after consulting a well-known biologist connected with the research station, that the eager little beavers had flooded the area very shallowly, not enough to destroy the lower plant life, such as the rare pitcher plant and other semiaquatic plants.

The beavers have built their homes in this shallow water, of mud and debris. Having an underwater entrance, they construct a narrow passageway to a "drying-off room," and their living quarters, just a little above the waterline, are moss-lined and really quite comfortable.

You see, the idea of building in the water is for protection and highly successful. Reckon they're just about the smartest small animal we have. They don't have much use for humans, though. One of the neighbors,

From left: Dick Meacham, Sarah Helen Meacham, Ricky Meacham, Harry Hill, Helen Hill Norris, Colonel James H. Howe, Lise Courtney Howe, Willet Sloan, Hazel Hill Sloan, and Maxie the dog in Horse Cove. *Courtesy of Robin Phillips.*

coming across a partly gnawed-down tree where they were building a dam, gave the tree a lick or two with his double-bitted axe and let it fall across the creek, thinking he'd help 'em along a little, I reckon. Blest if the whole colony of beavers didn't hump up and get mad and move out, lock, stock, and barrel, to their present colonized location.

HISTORY: HUDSON FREE LIBRARY

Even in the hurly-burly year of 1962, memories come flooding in. And with the Hudson Library's annual Silver Tea coming up, I can't help but remember Mother's account of the library's small but interesting beginning.

The tea, by the way, will be held at that very unusual, beautiful home perched high up on Little Bear Pen Mountain, the residence of Mrs. George Nathan. With its far-reaching views and interesting architecture, it presents a totally individual picture both inside and out, and the library group is most happy to have Mrs. Nathan's home for the gathering of its patrons and friends.

The Hudson Library had its beginning through a benevolent-minded, cultured woman from Boston, a Mrs. Hudson, mother of Mrs. Wells, who with her family pioneered here along with the New England colony long 'bout 1880.

The Wells family built their home over in Shortoff, and Mother said they played a large part in the development of cultural influences and of educational, religious, and social functions through the young town's early years.

Mrs. Hudson, being a friend of several Boston educators and writers, among them Edward Everett Hale, wasted no time at all in securing their interest for books in the newfound home.

So it came about that the Boston folk wrote her that they had selected several boxes of very fine books that they were shipping down. In those days, every single thing coming up here had to be hauled up over muddy, rocky, really bad roads in covered wagons called freighters. Joey Lovingood, that very picturesque team driver who figured in several accounts heretofore published, including Highlands' famous Whiskey War, was picked out to bring the big boxes up from the Seneca express office and was given sundry dire warnings as to what would happen to him if anything should happen to the library books.

Reckon poor old Joey imbibed a little too much on the way back, as how the back axle broke plumb in two coming up Pine Mountain, holding him up a day or two down there at the old Winchester place.

Anyway, seems the books, sent out with such loving care from Boston, arrived a pretty sorry-looking mess.

The late Professor T.G. Harbison of Pennsylvania—the father of our present efficient librarians, Dorothea and Gertrude Harbison—was the principal of the school then. With his customary habit of direct action, he declared school closed for two days, and all upper grades or classes were to come to the aid of the library books and save 'em!

Here came the Wells family, Mrs. Hudson, Mother and Dad—that was when they were young and gay—and both my grandfathers. Such a brushing away of damp and mold, spreading the books to dry out in the bright sunlight. They were so enthused that, before too long, when Mr. Harbison said more books were coming, the men hopped in and, with our professor in charge, built onto the schoolhouse a cute little many-windowed room. It was chestnut-paneled and lined with shelves. They put all three of the teachers cataloguing the books in proper order, and with Miss Alberta Staub as acting librarian, the Hudson Free Library was born.

It was opened generally once a week. On Friday afternoons, the ringing of the school bell announced to the populace that the library was open. Sometimes I get to thinking about how much cooperative strength there was in those early Highlanders. Seemed to be the sort of folk who made up their minds what they wanted and went after it tooth and nail.

As far back as then, Highlands had a wonderful glee club. It used to meet twice a month, generally at the George Kibbee home, now the residence of Mrs. J.A. Hines. There'd be an amateur string band, a debating group among the men over national issues, recitations of prose and poetry, and amusing themes acted out in pantomime by Dr. Kibbee's daughter Kitty. Dr. Kibbee, by the way, a typical Massachusetts Cape Codder, later became a tragic figure, when he volunteered his medical services and lost his life fighting the terrible yellow fever epidemic down in New Orleans back in the 1880s.

It's mighty fine to have a library like ours. I was in there only yesterday, browsing through the bookshelves and amusedly watching the bright-eyed children coming in and going out, some of them eagerly asking Miss Harbison for some special book. The Hudson Library means a lot to Highlands.

Malviny Sets Her House in Order

Seems the old home down here in the Cove has a way of luring folks to drop by. Sometimes there's a group of little folks, dark-eyed and flaxen-haired, on errands for their mother, expecting a cookie or two. And there's the kinfolks from far off and nigh, some of whom used to come for a "civil war" in the old days for a visit of from two to three weeks to three months. They were always welcome, but now in these busy days and days of swift transportation, they stop by for only a few hours or possibly an overnight visit. And last but not least are our friends from town. It's mighty nice.

Came a body the other day, a woman who intrigued me to no end. A type born to the wilderness and wilderness ways. A type of pioneer woman rapidly passing, I'm sorry to say, from the American scene.

Well poised and quietly dressed she was, and I asked her to rest a while and have a glass of iced tea. She explained that she was Mrs. Teague and was only passing by and thought she would stop and talk a while. She wanted to know if I was the "lady who writes for the paper."

"Yes'm," I says, "reckon so."

"Looks like you'd run out o' somethin' to write about," she went on. We sat quietly for a spell, listening to the bobwhite's call out in the evening-shadowed meadow, and as the sun lowered in the west back of Playmore, the Monroe place, I somehow sensed that this caller of mine had something important she wanted to say.

Folding her hands and gazing off into the sunset, she suddenly said, "You could write about Malviny Reid's 'bad spell.'"

"Well," I 'lowed, "folks been having 'bad spells' ever since I can remember, and besides, folks don't like to read about 'bad spells' very much."

"I dunno," she said, "reckon mebbe you'd better hear about Malviny. She was sure she was a-dyin. She was 'took' sudden, and it's no wonder, with her allus a-tearin' 'round, workin'. Hardes' workin' woman I ever saw. A passel o' us women, hearin' she was sick, jus' dropped by sort of neighborly-like since we think a lot o' Malviny an' her two grown girls. Well, she was layin' propped up in bed, lookin' pretty peaked, but I knowed the minute I laid eyes on her she was as mad as a hatter.

"'You can clear out,' she 'lowed to me and Mrs. Wilson and Mrs. Thomas. You know, Mrs. Thomas is sort of special 'cause her husband always spoke out in a meetin', and led in prayer in church. 'Yes, you can clear out,' she says. 'I got things to tend to for I'm a fixin' to die and ain't got much time left.'

"Well," my visitor says, "we just sort of tiptoed out, me an' the others, kind of ashamed for having come. I slipped back by the garden an' dug some taters and took 'em by the spring branch an' washed 'em, then I picked and shucked some roastin' ears to help the girls out. The door was open when I went back by the house, an' I'm telling you, Malviny was in there propped up in bed just a-layin' it on the line to the girls.

"'You two get busy now,' she says, 'and clean up and wind out this house good from top to bottom. I want every curtain took down an' washed, starched, and ironed, windows washed, inside an' out, air and sun the feather beds, an' wash the quilts and bedspreads. You got to bring some sand from the creek an' mix it with 'bout a gallon o' that homemade soap out in a barrel in the smokehouse, an' take the shuck broom an' scrub and scour the kitchen floor, tables, chairs, an' all. Better cook up a passel o' food, too. Lot o' people will be here to my buryin', and you, Hattie, bein' as how you're the oldest daughter an' particular like, I want you to go to my bureau drawers, clean 'em out an' reline 'em with fresh paper. That long-nosed sister of your pa's an' her outfit will be here, pokin' 'round in everything I've got, an' I sure aim to die with my house in order. Now GIT! Don't set there lookin' at me that away. Dyin's not so bad anyway when you've done the best you could all your life. I'm not aimin' or calculatin' on doin' any explainin' to the good Lord. He'll know.'"

The sun had gone down now beyond the distant mountain's rim, leaving a filtered glow of rose and purple falling on the meadows and a sort of a mist followed the valley's main stream down to the waterfall.

We sat quietly for a few minutes. I was waiting for my visitor to continue. Finally, she said, "You know Jed, my man, an' our neighbors an' me allus took care of our folks when they pass on. Always have, from way back. Never did calculate it was decent to call in an undertaker from town like most folks do now. Jus' don't seem 'fitten' somehow. So I hurried on home an' told Jed about Malviny a-fixin' to die, an' Jed 'lows, 'Well if she' fixin' to die, she means to. That old woman ain't never failed at nothin' she ever undertook. So me an' the menfolks'll get busy an' get that walnut lumber out o' the barn loft an' make her a real coffin.' Looked real nice it did, too, all sanded down smooth an' varnished. They'd gone to the hardware store in Walhalla for some silver-lookin' handles. Real nice."

"I know the rest of the story, Mrs. Teague," I says. "Malviny, for all her planning to die, up and got well."

"That's what she did, sure as God made little green apples," my caller said. "Made us all 'bout half mad, too, after we'd gone to all that trouble,

From left: Sally Lee Phillips, Sally Sloan Phillips, Robin Phillips, Dorothy Norris Turner, and Helen Jeanne Turner at Peggy Hole in Horse Cove. *Courtesy of Robin Phillips.*

much less the menfolks takin' time off from pullin' fodder to make her as nice a coffin as a body's want.

"'Twas plumb inconsiderate of Malviny, that's what it was. An' you know somethin', them men, after Malviny was up and around, got scared to death she'd find out 'bout that coffin and lay 'em out, and that coffin's up in the barn loft over at Sam's house, hid out."

So still now, the evening, as I watched my interesting visitor wind her way homeward, leaving me to ponder over the great individualism and human-interest lore that abounds in these glorious mountains of ours.

EXPERIENCE OF THE POST OFFICE INSPECTOR

Long time ago, before the Rural Free Delivery system came in, small post offices were scattered here and there through the countryside, often in remote sections. Once in a while came the official postal inspector from Washington, checking.

He was a personal friend of my folks down on the farm, and Dad and Mother were often highly entertained by the inspector's experiences. One time he stayed over a day or two on account of heavy rains and swollen mountain streams, which had to be forded. He drove a horse and buggy, and his name was Mr. Harshburger.

He'd been over in the Sapphire country somewhere this particular visit, going over the accounts in a small office in the store of a Mr. Albright. He was a conscientious and gentle person but unpredictable; seems he was given to opening his post office and store according to conditions generally and the weather.

It was bitter cold that January, and Mr. Harshburger, finding the little store with its post office closed, figured he'd ask around and try to locate the missing entrepreneur. He found out that he had not been seen or heard from for days, but finding out from a feller he met up with where Mr. Albright's home was located, way up a little-used road two or three miles away, Mr. Harshburger took off, driving along a little meandering stream that served as a road guide.

In a little while he came to a tree that had fallen across the road, and after taking his axe and chopping his way around the tree, he finally came in view of the house he was looking for. It had smoke coming from the chimney, so he figured the keeper of Uncle Sam's mail was at home.

They "chewed the rag" for a while, sort of passing the time o' day—weather conditions, etc. Mr. Harshburger by long experience and contacts knew that no local person ever, under any circumstances, stated the object of his business first off. But finally he comes out with the statement, "I see you've closed the post office at Painter Town, Mr. Albright."

"No, I ain't to say closed it," says the postmaster. "Just sort of suspended it, you might say. My old woman took to the bed with the flu, then I took sick, and what with the big tree falling across the road in the last big ice storm and freeze, an' nobody to get wood and tote water or feed the stock, an' both of us down in the bed, when I took down sick, I just naturally took off and packed that post office on my back up here."

"But then where is the Painter Town post office now?" Mr. Harshburger inquired.

"It's right here, safe and sound, right under my bed," Mr. Albright answered. "That's where it is, an' that's where it's goin' to stay 'til the weather and me gets better."

Mr. Harshburger said they pulled the boxes out and he sat down and made his report—the records were as neatly kept as any he'd ever seen—after which the old couple begged him to stable his horse, have supper with them, and turn in for the night. This he was glad to do, for as the postmaster allowed, "it was a spittin' snow out of the northwest, and it was bitter cold."

Soon there was a delicious smell of frying homemade sausage, hot biscuits, and coffee, and the bemused, somewhat exhausted gentleman from Washington slept the winter's night through 'neath a sloping roof in the attic.

Once during the night, long 'bout two o'clock in the morning, he allowed that he heard a wild and alarming scream coming from above on the mountain. He hit the floor with a bang, upon which his host called up the ladder that was tacked to the side of the wall in the room below. "You don't need to be nary a bit scared, Mr. Harshburger," Mr. Albright said. "It ain't nothin' but a 'painter cat.'" (A panther, that is.)

GRANDMOTHERS

It's a strange, sort of mysterious silence—a hushed sort of silence—one feels upon waking up early on a mountain winter's morning to find the majestic conifers and hardwoods blanketed overnight in snow. So silently it came, the snow—no wind, maybe a filtered gentle whisper now and then on a window pane—that drawing aside the curtains in the morning light, there it lies in all its silent and beautiful majesty.

Then, too, most always, in climbing to the top of a lofty peak, a hushed sort of feeling—the silence again, inexplicable and restful. And last but not least, the noonday silence falling 'neath the lofty pines and hemlock boughs in the dense forest, when even the songs of our shyest birds are stilled. Sometimes one wonders. It could be Nature's tribute, the majestic silences, to the Creator of our marvelous world.

Used to be, come Labor Day, with September's golden shadowed sunlight, our "summer people," as we were wont to call our lowland visitors, left early, along with our birds, and a dead silence fell alike on hill and dale. And even Main Street was a lonely spot.

Things have changed, what with the rapid transit by air and by motorcars. Our visitors come and go, always coming for the Indian blanket colors that turn the great forests into a blaze of riotous color come October.

Reckon I fell to thinking about this silence business was on account of paying a sort of unexplained tribute, mentally speaking, to grandmothers in general. And remembering, now that I am a grandmother myself, how with great conceit of a young mother here, I'd come blithely up from South Carolina with my four "darlings," saying how lovely it was for dear Mother and Dad to have said "darlings" come for all summer—such a ridiculous ego!

Helen Hill Norris, *center*, with, *from left*, her children Frank Norris, Helen Norris Flippin, Jack Norris, and Dorothy Norris Turner. *Courtesy of Helen Hill Norris family.*

How in the world Mother and Dad stood it I don't know. What with four-year-old Jack, being unusually quiet one busy morning, proceeding to take a dipper, and with the stock pantry door shut, quietly and carefully mixing a barrel of salt with a barrel of sugar. And the same summer, one of the young'uns picking up the yellow kitten and dropping him into the butter churn, 'lowing as how the kitten now could be christened "Butter Ball."

Those parents, though, bless 'em, took it all on the chin. Not a word of exasperation. But I know, and know full well, that the calm and silence following the September flight southward of "darlings" was one of thankful relief.

The "Order of Grandmothers" still exists. One sees and meets them over and over in the shops about town, and in the riding stables where they sit quietly reading or knitting while "small fry" ride around and around our enclosed and prescribed circle for hours on end.

One sometimes hears or overhears one patient grandmother saying to another patient grandmother, "Yes, I have Marion's children this summer, and their dogs and pet mice. You see," not missing a lick of her busy knitting, "Marion and Ted are on a western tour and are looking in on the world's fair in Seattle. Then when they return to Highlands, they're bringing a group of their friends and their children, maybe some more dogs, too."

They're really wonderful, the O.G. (Organization of Grandmothers). Maybe unhonored and unsung. Bless 'em.

But come September's golden silence and the return of the little darlings to school and kindergarten, there'll be a needed rest, perhaps, as a lonely grandmother misses the patter of little feet and endless demands on her time and loving care.

HORSE COVE ROAD

The road twisted and turned, almost meeting itself on many a hairpin curve. It wasn't a road, really, just a trace in the early 1800s. It followed its older brother, the Indian trail, southward and was marked now and then by a "blazed" tree. It meandered down the forested and steep mountainside, a trail that had once known only the soft tread of the moccasined feet of America's vanishing race, the Indians.

It was growing dark, and the big drove of turkeys the boy had been driving for many days from way over beyond the Smokies, from the rich valleys of the Tennessee country's lush farmlands, were tired. The boy was tired, too, and the big lead gobbler, carrying his little turkey bell around his neck, was looking for a place to roost for the night among the age-old tall pines and hemlocks. The flock of turkeys, sometimes as many as two hundred of them, followed the sound of his tinkling bell.

The turkeys gave the boy no trouble as he drove them along the devious route to the markets in the lowlands. This was the day of the drovers.* There was no other way then for the transportation of livestock, and amusedly, the drovers were a class to themselves, for those who drove the great, fine, high-stepping Tennessee walking horses were rather picturesque figures, with their polished boots and better greatcoats. They sort of high-hatted the drovers of the cattle, hogs, sheep, and turkeys and were often entertained by the gentry down in Charleston at the end of their long trek.

"Someday," the boy thought as he fell asleep by his campfire, wrapped in his blanket with the silent, guarding forest around him, "someday I will be a grand horse drover, too, and maybe there'll even be a fine road here, all paved over like a feller hears about in the big cities out beyond. People will be driving big Conestoga wagons like they're making up in Pennsylvania. Maybe there will even be fine carriages, too, and fine, sleek horses with brass-trimmed harnesses. Could be."

---

* A drover is a person who drives cattle or sheep to market.

Trail trees, or blaze trees, were trees that the Cherokees bent to mark turns on a trail.
Courtesy of Robin Phillips.

And he slept then, with the dreamless comfort of a well-spent day behind and many more ahead.

I like to take that road now, sometimes walking the three and a half miles. It is a picturesque road, with the primeval forest that falls a thousand feet in three miles from the Ravenel Gap just beyond the Highlands city limits to the level valley of Horse Cove. Each turn of the road recalls the days of following at Grandpa's heels when he would tell me little happenings, when as a young surveyor, coming from over in Rutherford County, he laid out the road following the Indian trail. I reckon it's kind of remarkable that the road still follows, with one exception, the same grade and route.

"There's Billy Dismal," he'd say. Billy, being the first white man to settle in the Cove, was a powerful hunter and trapper. He set his bear trap out there once where the big cliff breaks off. He came along going over his trap line one day. Seeing his trap held in its savage grip a panther, and realizing that he'd left his gun at home, he grabbed a big stout chunk o' wood, aimin' to lay his "painter" out pronto. Reckon he'd underestimated the length of the chain fastened to the trap, 'cause the "painter," intent on big business, sprung at him. Billy turned to run, leaving the entire backside of his pants with the panther. Tale is, Billy walked all the way home "hindside-fore," 'fraid he'd meet somebody in the road.

"Pretty embarrassed Billy was, I reckon," says Grandpa. "He's been Billy Dismal ever since."

I remember coming then to the rock quarry, 'bout halfway where Grandpa had entered a claim back when he first came. Back then, one had only to file a claim in Raleigh with a $1.50 fee and fence in a log cabin and the state would grant him a deed. Jim Henry, who was Grandfather's right-hand helper, lived there once, the cabin long since burned. Jim, whom Grandfather loved, lies buried on the high ridge above the rock quarry, his grave marked by his children and his grandchildren. Jim was at work on the road one day when he struck a glancing blow with his mattock against an outcrop of solid granite, and out poured in slivery brilliance a spring of water.

He was so surprised he yelled, "Squire!" Everybody called Grandpa "Squire," seemed like. "Run here right quick, Squire!" Jim yelled.

When Grandpa looked, he said to Jim, "We'll call it Moses Rock, Jim. Remember, I always want it called Moses Rock from now on, because in the Old Testament, where Moses was leading the children of Israel, and they were tired and thirsty, somewhere it says that Moses smote the rock and there was water for all."

Well, Moses Rock is still there on the roadside. We keep thinking when we travel the road that we'll get around to placing a marker by it, but somehow we never have.

Then, 'round a bend or two farther along, I remember riding down the mountain from town on my horse with my baby Frank held in front of me on the saddle, hearing our dogs treeing something by the road. Knowing by the way they'd close in and jump back from the bank that it was a snake, and knowing that our dogs never fooled around with anything but a rattler, I turned my horse around, tied him to a bush, and put my baby up on the high bank. I took the stoutest stick I could lay hands on and went back and killed the biggest and meanest rattlesnake I've ever run across, trying at the same time to keep the dogs from getting bitten. I then tied the snake to my saddle. I remember he dragged the ground. Then I picked up my baby and started home.

When I rode into the yard, Dad says, "Is that a rattlesnake you've got tied there?"

"Yes sir," I says. "I killed him up at Moses Rock, and 'lowed as how none of you would believe how big he is, I brought him home."

"Never," says Dad, "did I think I'd raise a child with as little sense. Don't you know it's a thousand wonders that horse, as fractious as he is, didn't run away with that snake dangling there like that?" He then reached up and took the baby, his namesake, safely in his arms, leaving me with something to think about.

It's a dear road. When one takes time to walk it, one can let time turn backward. The singing little brooklets on their merry way to the sea are bridged and culverted now, where once we let the checkreins down for our horses to drink. A road that maybe remembers once only the tread of moccasined feet of the Cherokee and the calls of the drovers along the trace.

UNCLE BOBBY'S STORE

Uncle Bobby kept a store over in Cashiers Valley. That was a long time ago.

Kept near about everything a body would need, I reckon, from cornshuck horse collars and plough points and sticky fly paper to a brace of ladies' hats hanging yearly behind a glass-enclosed wall cabinet. Each year they'd appear, those hats, come spring. That they finally became sadly flyspecked and beribboned and beflowered crowns and brims, rather tired looking, mattered not at all to me when I'd go sometimes with Dad. Always there was a silent determination that when I became a young lady I'd buy one of those hats!

That day it was cold, I remember. Dad was having a ball with Uncle Bobby, talking over politics and passing the time of day 'bout one thing and another while I tried on, at Mother's suggestion, my first pair of patent leather pumps behind the counter.

Here come busting in what looked to me like a dozen young'uns, all ages and sizes, and such a scrambling into things: candy counter, chewing gum, soft drink chest.

"Looks like, Bob, these young'uns are going to walk off with your store," says Dad.

Without saying nary a word, up rose Uncle Bobby, reaching for a rack of long shiny-looking buggy whips overhead. (Remember, they had fine red-and-yellow silk tassels on their tips.) He gave about ten licks right and left, and out through doors and windows went Uncle Bobby's children and grandchildren, and still he never said a word to them nor lost one word of what Dad was saying.

Front row, from left: Willet Sloan, Sally Sloan Phillips with Sally Lee Phillips on her lap, Helen Russell, and Frank H. Hill. *Back row, from left*: Stacey Russell and three unidentified women. Photo taken in 1944. *Courtesy of Robin Phillips.*

Action without words. He was a fine gentleman, though, Uncle Bobby—typically Irish, but little or no chance of anything resembling an education, even of the most elementary sort.

Came a feller in a little later saying he'd come by to settle up his bill at the store. Reached down on a lower shelf for his account book, Uncle Bobby did, and turning through the pages marked a place, saying, "Yeah, here is a Tom. Owe me for a whole ten-pound box of that Michigan hoop cheese."

Looking over his shoulder at the book, Tom says, "H'come a cheese? I ain't never bought a whole cheese in my life, 'cept 'bout a pound or two maybe once in a while. Sides, there ain't no writin' or figgers here, nothin' but a picture of some awful-lookin' thing—looks like a wagon wheel, sort of. H'come there ain't no writin' or figgers about what I owe you, Uncle Bobby?"

With a certain dignity, that dear storekeeper said, "Well, Tom, you ought to know by this time I can't read or write. So when folks buy anything and don't pay for it when they get it, I just take out this old book o' mine and draw me a pitcher of it. Now this big round thing I drawed here with a hole in the center is 'bliged to be a cheese. It's got a cross mark by it, which is your mark, and if it ain't a cheese, what is it?"

"Shucks," said Tom, "that's easy. I bought a fourteen-inch grindstone from you last March to set up longside my barn at the watering trough to sharpen my axe and mowing blades on. That's what that is, and here's your $1.50."

Listening, I concluded that an education could be a pretty useful thing after all.

CROSSING THE CREEK

While the north winds come roaring in from over the mountains to the northwest and rattle the windows, our beautiful village lies calm under the brittle frost, with its four beautiful church spires making a picture against an open azure sky—a moonlit sky at night—a "skiff" of snow accenting the fir tree.

I sort of started remembering how Dad never killed hogs 'til just before Christmas, no matter what. I reckon there being no such commodities as a deep freeze, refrigeration, etc., one had to depend on real cold weather for curing the meat. Anyway, Mother and us young'uns all deplored it. It made such a mess right at Christmas.

Come Christmas Eve one year, I'm remembering, it was cold as kraut, and we young'uns began to think it was a poor outlook for the main holiday of the year, what with the big long table on the screened back porch plumb full of frozen hog heads waiting to be cleaned and made into pressed meat, sausage to be ground, etc. That little old black iron sausage mill looked exactly like a miniature old-time coal- or wood-burning locomotive that used to run on the Tallulah Falls Railway! The meat hopper where the meat went in on top was like a smokestack, but my, oh my, what luscious sausage it turned out, seasoned with Mother's homegrown sage.

Long 'bout two o'clock that Christmas Eve, I 'lowed to the others, "Ain't nothin' to this. It's Christmas, and Mother and Dad are in a 'swivet' over the bloomin' hog killin'. Let's go!"

So off with a double-bitted axe and hatchet across the Thompsons' swamp in front of Hill House, across the creek where Mrs. Howe's beaver dams are now, on to the pine forest on the slopes of Rich Mountain, where we cut a lovely tree. Then we loaded our feed sack with red-berried holly and started back across the creek, which was up— way up—and most out of its banks. The slim pole that served as a foot log was swaying above a swift current and, to me, with my Christmas tree and axe, it began to look like a problem to make it across.

The small fry, carrying the holly, "cooned" it across by straddling the log and humping themselves along.

Full of advice to me after they'd made it across, they said, "Maybe you'd better wait for us to go for Dad."

"No," I says. "I can't ford it with the tree and the axe, that's for sure, but don't go for Dad. He's allus in a bad humor anyway when he's got a lot to do 'round the place, and he's nervous over getting the meat cured and all."

It was then I remembered Calloway McCall, who used to help Dad around the place, and how he said he once came down the "cat stairs" into the gorge where the east prong of the Chattooga River was crossed on a foot log. On his way to town he was, with a ten-gallon keg o' molasses on his back and two bundles of fodder for a cow that was pastured across the river. He was taking the molasses to his daughter, who lived across the Jackson County line. He said the river was up and the foot log was treacherously smooth. He crossed it, he said, by taking a "run and go."

So I took off in high gear, tree, axe, and all. 'Bout middleways across all, of a sudden I *knew* I was going to fall in! Down into the icy current I went, the tree and me a swirling mass. But hanging on to my Christmas tree, I caught hold of a bunch of leaning alder bushes and finally got up and out and across. Then, in less than a minute, it seemed, my red flannel dress was frozen stiff, and the tree full of icy crystals.

We got home in no time at all, though, and soon I was changing into warm, dry clothing. Then very shortly afterward, the tree was in the big bay window, and Mother was putting the white-winged angel on top and the little red candles in the tin holders. Then we decorated the house with the red-berried holly, over mirrors, doorways, and mantel. It was beautiful!

"Surely," Mother said as she went to the kitchen to finish frying her delicious New England doughnuts, "surely, my dears, Christmas belongs to the country."

THE THREE-MONTHS SCHOOL

We've been "burning our candle at both ends. It scarce will last throughout the night. But oh! My foes and oh! My friends, it gives a lovely light."*

What with the happy holidays, which we southerners have a way of copying from Merrie Old England's custom of "keeping" the Twelve Days of Christmas, as told in that fascinating ballad by the same title (long forgotten until some smart feller resurrected it from the dusty files in the "Auld Countrie" and recorded it), we "inlanders" do have a merrie old time in the winter. No doubt of it. There's been kinfolk coming and going, spend-the-day parties, friends in for a five o'clock. It's all very gay!

Then there's the frozen lakes making a picture at night, with the skaters in their bright-colored woolens, the bright-colored lights criss-crossing and reflecting from the silvered beauty below, and bonfires along the shoreline lighting up a background of age-old hemlock and pine standing solemnly on guard. Yes, it's a lovely scene.

During a fireside chit-chat with the folks one evening, I fell to thinking about the old school days and of how we only had three months of school in our tucked-away hills and valleys. It began in September and wound up long about the first of December with what was known as an "entertainment." And that was no small affair! Tradition from way back, time out of mind, says that the teacher was supposed to, and had better be prepared to, "treat"—candy, fruit, nuts, etc.

We talked about those olden days for a while, and then Thelma spoke up and 'lowed as how, when she was teaching down in Horse Cove, she went

---

* "My candle burns at both ends; / It will not last the night; / But ah, my foes, and oh, my friends; / It gives a lovely light!" ("First Fig," by the poet Edna St. Vincent Millay, 1920).

Horse Cove School, 1898. *From left*: Leonard Hill, Genelia Speed, Sallie Wilson, Lena Wilson, Mary Edwards, Simon Speed, Hoyt Hill (small boy), Carrie Edwards, Radford Hill, Edna McKinney, John Edwards, Barnett Wilson, Garse Edwards and Lafayette Speed. The small girl in front of Lafayette may be one of the Wilson children. Fannie McKinney is the teacher. *Courtesy of Helen Hill Norris family.*

to the door during a morning arithmetic class when she heard a commotion out in the road. Seems it was a neighbor from over toward Whiteside Cove who was holding on to a three-month-old shoat,* which he was driving by the simple means of a rope tied to the pig's hind leg. The pig was of course objecting vigorously and vociferously!

Well, anyway, the man called out, "Thelma, when do you aim to have your school entertainment? I got to drive this here shoat plumb down to Cashiers Valley, and I 'lowed as how I'd 'norate' the word about your 'entertainment' as I went. Everybody ought to know about it."

Poor old Thelma, how on earth did she ever put on such a play! Laboring with one of her fourteen-year-old boys, creating a romantic Romeo, making his impassioned and famous ode to the fair Juliet in the balcony scene from Shakespeare's famous play.

She made a "borrow" of Mother's hall chandelier of antique rose and brass. Mother was terribly apprehensive for fear it would be broken as they

---

* A young, weaned pig.

all made off up the cottage hill with it. True, they did fall down with it but managed to save it from breaking. Two of the school trustees managed a stage, a fine curtain was rigged up somehow or other, and the children's mothers managed fairly presentable costumes from boxes of secondhand clothing from the King's Daughters thrift store, sent down from Boston. The play was so successful it was for a long time the topic of neighborhood talk.

Dad, teaching his first school down Clear Creek after graduating from college, remembered how the boys came near to getting the best of him at school closing time. He allowed as how, what with the school entertainment that night and plenty of food, there would be no treat from the teacher at the school closing. He reckoned he'd underestimated the resourcefulness of his student body, because the morning of the last day, arriving at the schoolhouse, he was amazed to find no pupils and the door barred hard and fast. When he heard an explosive sound of laughter coming from the wooded backyard, Dad knew he was in for some trouble and determined to outwit them at their own game.

He proceeded to "hist" himself up the stick-and-mud chimney and come down, landing in the fireplace inside. Again he was outsmarted, 'cause he landed smack-dab onto a bed of hot coals, from which he beat a hasty retreat back up the chimney.

"All right, fellows, I give up," he yelled. "Two of you hustle over to the store and bring back this list of treats."

And so, somewhat disheveled and sooty, the teacher of the Clear Creek School closed the school good-naturedly, and maybe a little proud of his pupils' prowess in outsmarting him.

THE WARWOMAN

They're a type to themselves, always have been and still are, the women of the mountains. With their aptitude for quick thinking and acting, especially in the emergencies that evolved by necessity in their forebears, they have long been a source of admiration to close observers.

It was a day for remembering. A May day it was, and out across the hills and dales, the dainty bluebells of Robert Burns's* Scotland, and the fragile service trees were abloom, a fairy-like beauty against a backdrop of delicate green leafing.

---

* Robert Burns (1759–1796) is considered the national poet of Scotland.

Down in the Warwoman Country, just across the Georgia line from Pine Mountain over to Clayton, lies an interesting sort of place. It holds within its sheltered coves and hills the life story of many of the very first pioneers. Can't help but comment just here, though, that nowhere I've ever been—West, East, or North—do I fail to find much that I'd like to write about, all up and down the Mississippi and then way out beyond to the Pacific Ocean, the fun I've had talking to people and digging up local stories!

Warwoman Country is picturesque as it leads in and out among gentle rises of land and fertile little bottomlands along Warwoman Creek. It's not as rugged and spectacular as our own proud Highlands Plateau. Warwoman Country is quite peaceful now compared to the hair-raising days of the early 1800s.

Easter, who came every Monday to do our washing, was from Warwoman Country. I've mentioned her before. She was an intelligent woman, and we used to love to hear her tell how her folks came from Pennsylvania over the Wilderness Trail. Seems to me now as I write this, she'd mention her grandfather traveling along with Daniel Boone so casually. How I wish I had written down all the things she used to tell us. Anyway, we young'uns knew that when she got the fire going good under the big washpot and had her first tub full of clothes boiling away, she'd be good for a tale.

One day when I asked her how come it was called Warwoman, she said, "Indians named her."

"Yeah, but how come?" I insisted.

"The Cherokee Indians were treated mighty bad, honey, and don't you ever forget it," she said. "Lots of people coming in from across the big waters and running Indians off and taking their lands. The Indians down there in Warwoman Country were fighting back pretty strong, so that my mother and grandmother carried guns even to go to the spring and back. The menfolks even took guns to the Meetin' House."

I was completely fascinated by Easter's tale by this time and begged her to continue.

"Well," she said, "Grandma Nicholson was going about her housework one morning, a day like this in May. She was singing that sweet old song that came across the big waters—'Barbara Allen,'* I think it was—and she had put a big pot full of homemade lye soap on in the fireplace to boil. We made our own soap then, honey; no store-bought lye, either, like now. The lye was run off from the oak ashes burned in the fireplace in an ash hopper out in the yard, generally a hollowed-out tree trunk set up on a little platform.

---

* A traditional English ballad.

When it was about full, Grandpa would pour water in and let it seep down and run out a little trough at the bottom of the hopper into a tub. It was mixed with a soap grease from a big jar that we kept for scrap meat and fat stuff, and it'd make the best soap a body ever used, and it cost nothin' but a little hard work."

Easter punched down the pot full of clothes as she went on with her tale.

"The children were playin' around the door in the yard that day in May, and everything seemed peaceful when suddenly Grandpa Nicholson grabbed his muzzle-loading rifle from over the door and yelled, 'Grab, the young'uns and run. Indians! Bill Scroggins just come by and said he seen 'em over at Chunky Gal Mountain with guns and tomahawks.'

"Grandma got busy right quick and covered up the fire under her soap pot," she continued, "first testing the strength of the soap with the long-handled gourd used for a dipper. Then, calmly and quietly, she got the children together and took off with the rest of her neighbors out across the creek toward South Carolina. Reckon they made camp long toward nightfall, and the next morning, Grandma Nicholson, remembering her soap pot, and being young and strong and fearless, took off back home in spite of dire warnings from the others. She was thinking only of her precious soap and the cow waiting to be milked. The chickens also had to be fed. As she took off in high feather, she laughingly said she'd be back by evening.

"Well," Easter went on, "Grandma Nicholson found everything all right when she got there, so she unchained the cabin doors and started to get things going. While bending over the fire, she all at once knew there was someone standing in the doorway. Maybe a shadow fell across the floor. Without raising up and without making a speck o' noise, she reached up by the fireboard for the long-handled gourd, which held a good quart of that hot boiling soap. Before you could even think, she flung it at the big Cherokee Indian standing in the doorway! Letting out a yell of 'Wah-loo-hee'—Cherokee for 'war woman'—he was gone. But by that time, another Indian was coming toward her from the open back door with his tomahawk raised, and *slap-dab*, he got his quart of hot liquid, and he, too, went off screaming into the forest.

"When the folks came back next day, there stood Grandma, laughing fit to kill and sort of lording it over the menfolks, who were a little shame-faced, I reckon, when they found out that one lone little woman had run off a whole batch of Indians. The tracks of their moccasined feet and the pony tracks showed that there was a considerable bunch of 'em.

From the *Daily Mail* newspaper of Anderson, South Carolina, January 2, 1901: "Wedding in Anderson Most Novel on Record: At St. John's Methodist church Monday night 'watch night' services were held and a large concourse of people witnessed the dying of the old year and 19th century and the ushering in of the new year and 20th century. The feature of the program was the marriage of John J. Norris of this city and Miss Helen Hill of Horse Cove N.C. which began at 11:57 and closed three minutes after 12:00. Rev. J.B. Campbell performed the ceremony, and the plucky bride and groom were wedded under circumstances that can never exist again in a hundred years. The groom is the son of Capt. P.K. Norris, one of the most prominent citizens of this place. He is highly esteemed, a young man of noble character, and is an electrician at Orr cotton mills. The bride is the daughter of Mr. Frank Hill of Horse Cove N.C. She is cultured and attractive and her friends are numerous." *Courtesy of Helen Hill Norris family.*

"It's been called 'Warwoman Country' ever since," said Easter, "and I reckon it always will be. Now git! And help me hang out this wash. Maybe next time I'll tell you about the Lost Gold Miner who disappeared and never was heard of again."

ABOUT THE AUTHOR

Helen Martense Hill Norris was born in Highlands, North Carolina, in 1882, one of four children of Sarah Frost Hill and Frank Harrison Hill. She and her husband, John J. Norris, had four children of their own and lived in South Carolina and Atlanta before returning to Highlands and her beloved Horse Cove valley. Known fondly to her family as Mama Helen, she was a naturally gifted storyteller. On warm summer evenings, her grandchildren, great-grandchildren, nieces, and nephews would gather on the porch of her family's Hill House estate in Horse Cove to listen as Mama Helen told stories of the joys, troubles, and adventures of growing up there in the late 1800s. She had an adventurous streak that she carried into adulthood, traveling cross-country to California in a Ford Model T, sailing to Europe with her two daughters on the *Queen Elizabeth*, and operating a successful antique shop in Atlanta. For a decade starting in 1958, she wrote a weekly column for the *Highlander* newspaper called "Looking Backward" in which she shared stories from her own childhood and those she had absorbed from her elders on cold nights huddled around the Hill House fireplace. A selection of these columns was collected in two volumes in 1962 and 1963, and they are being reprinted here in slightly edited form for the first time in nearly six decades. She died in 1968 and is buried in Horse Cove among many of the relatives whom she brought so vividly to life in her writing.

Visit us at
www.historypress.com